Praise for *Wild Card*

"The passion, creativity, and clever strategies displayed by Hope and Wade King in *The Wild Card* are inspiring. This book is a teacher wonderland of ideas, inspiration, and mind-blowing magic that impressed me beyond words. Hope and Wade have shown us all how to be better and hone our craft as educators. They have discovered a way to help all teachers reach their true potential and have enabled us all to inspire every child to achieve success.

—**Ron Clark**, *New York Times* bestselling author, founder, Ron Clark Academy

"Hope and Wade provide powerful, proven, practical steps to discovering the creativity inside us all. The Kings are master educators who engage, uplift, and challenge their students daily. They are the real deal, and they have managed to capture the hopes and the fears that every educator faces. Their words will leave you empowered and determined to find your own creative breakthrough."

—**Kim Bearden**, co-founder and executive director, Ron Clark Academy, National Hall of Fame Teacher of the Year, *LA Times* bestselling author of *Crash Course*

"*The Wild Card* is a phenomenal book that speaks directly to educators. The various approaches to challenges within the classroom are both accurate and relatable. Wade and Hope have done a fantastic job of addressing how we can provide realistic solutions by becoming *the Wild Card*!"

—**Leonard Galloway**, principal at Robert Anderson Middle School

"When was the last time your students got excited about worksheets? *Never!* That's because worksheets don't work, at least not when it comes to instilling a love for learning. In *The Wild Card*, Wade and Hope King challenge, equip, and emPOWER you to create lessons that bring light (not dread) to your students' eyes. The activities and lesson ideas in this book can be adapted for different subjects and grade levels and, most importantly, will have your students running to get into your class!"

—Jason David Frank, actor, legendary Power Ranger, Comic Icon, and seventh-degree black belt martial artist

"Just in the nick of time! With teacher shortages at an all-time high across the nation, *The Wild Card* provides future and current educators an opportunity to truly recognize the power they possess within, in order to reach and teach a generation longing for something different. Wade and Hope King's passion for developing exceptional instructional leaders in every area of their lives is felt with each turn of the page."

—Damon M. Qualls, elementary school principal and Call Me MiSTER Program Trailblazer, South Carolina Association for Supervision and Curriculum Development executive board member

"If you are an educator who desires to turn up the energy and engagement level of your class, this book is for you! If that desire isn't in you, it will be when you read this book. These pages are full of real-life stories that will pull you in and challenge you to your core. You will be motivated, inspired, and encouraged. Most of all, this book will help you quiet that little voice that tries to steal the joy out of shaping future generations through education."

—Amy Lemons, educator and blogger

"I always say that a teacher is someone who inspires, empowers, entertains, nurtures, counsels, consoles, and educates youth, and often all at the same time. This book encompasses all of that. When it comes to education, the messenger is so much more important than the message, and teaching is more about inspiration than information. Wade and Hope break down every aspect that an educator needs to become the teacher that students will never forget. *The Wild Card* is a manual for all teachers, whether it is your first year or fifteenth. This book reinforces that most successful educators possess three qualities: passion, compassion, and knowledge."

—**Nicholas Ferroni**, award-winning educator and activist

"Whether you're a brand-new teacher just starting out or an experienced veteran, *The Wild Card* has something for you. The passion Wade and Hope have for education shines through on every page. This book will encourage you to be a better teacher and to engage your students in high-quality instruction. Their insight to education inspires you to stretch your students and yourself, and the personal stories they share will make you smile as you turn the pages. Wade and Hope challenge us to see students as individuals with untapped potential and to look beyond the sum of their clothes, houses, and parent incomes. If you need a jumpstart in your classroom, this is the perfect book for you, as it offers ideas and excitement to engage your students."

—**Gerry Brooks**, elementary principal and social media educator personality

HOPE & WADE KING

THE
WILD
CARD

7 STEPS TO AN **EDUCATOR'S** CREATIVE BREAKTHROUGH

Wild Card

© 2017 by Wade King & Hope King

This book is available at special discounts when purchased in quantity for use as premiums, promotions, fundraisers, or for educational use. For inquiries and details, contact the publisher at books@daveburgessconsulting.com.

Published by Dave Burgess Consulting, Inc.
San Diego, CA
http://daveburgessconsulting.com

Cover Design by Genesis Kohler
Editing and Interior Design by My Writers' Connection

Library of Congress Control Number: 2017961374
Paperback ISBN: 978-1-946444-52-3
Ebook ISBN: 978-1-946444-53-0

First Printing: January 2018

Contents

INTRODUCTION . . . . **xi**

   Our Own Path xii

   Flexing the Creative Muscle xv

Part I: Wild Card **1**

Chapter One: The Game of Life **5**

   Creativity Is a Personal Brand 11

   Creativity Is a Mindset 13

   Creativity Drives Engagement 15

Chapter Two: The Deck is *Not* Stacked Against You **17**

Chapter Three: Don't Listen to the Joker **21**

   Change the Dialogue 23

   Shrug Off Setbacks 24

Part II: Creative Breakthrough **29**

Chapter Four: Awareness **37**

   Evaluate where you are today and accept it so you
   can move forward. 37

   Assess, Accept, Act 40

   What's Your WHY? 42

   Why You Need to Know Your Why 48

Chapter Five: Desire **53**

   Let desire drive your commitment to challenge yourself
   and step outside your comfort zone. 53

   Don't Live in the Comfort Zone 56

   First Step: A Smile. 61

   Rediscover Your Passion and Enthusiasm 64

   Fake It till You Make It. 68

Chapter six: Reflection. **73**

Reflect on your own creative path. What will it look like? 73

Consider New Definitions of Creativity. 75

Reflect on Your Vision for Change 77

Reflect on Your Goals. 81

Chapter Seven: Engagement **85**

Develop a new understanding of engagement. 85

The Rules of Rigor 88

Set Your *Expectations* High and Don't Accept Less. 91

Create an *Environment* that Furthers Your Goals 95

Maintain a High Level of *Energy*. *107*

Build a Culture of *Empowerment* *111*

Wrapping It All Together 120

Chapter Eight: Authenticity **123**

Identify your go-to thing and start there. 123

Getting Started 133

Leveling Up 139

Avoid the Comparison Trap 140

Ideas Everywhere! 143

Chapter Nine: Grit **153**

Push through barriers and overcome obstacles. 153

Crush Your Curriculum Challenges. 156

Trounce Those Testing Troubles 160

Bust Through Budget Boundaries 164

Work Through Personal Struggles with Self-Awareness. . .168

Chapter Ten: Persistence. **173**

Persist with and build on your creative efforts. 173

Try Something Beyond Your Go-To Thing. 175

Start a Club 176
Lift Up Your Colleagues 181

Chapter Eleven: Snappy Wrap-Up **185**

Part III: Toolbox **189**
Cheers and Chants / Call and Response 191
Relationships and Culture 192
Soft Skills 194
Movement 195
Music 196
Games / Competition 198
Current Events 199
Debate 201
Effective Questioning 203
STEM / STEAM 205
Socratic Seminar 206
Spoken Word 207
Drama / Role Play 208
Public Speaking 210
Room Transformation 211

Works Cited **225**

Acknowledgements **227**

More from Dave Burgess Consulting, Inc. **231**

About the Authors **242**

INTRODUCTION

We all know what creativity looks like, right? It's the bold colors and swirling brushstrokes on an expressionist canvas. It's those bestselling books that fly off the shelves to become epic films. Creativity shows in animatronic dinosaurs that roar and the cutting-edge lyrics to a blockbuster rap musical. It's even apparent in that wedding cake that's an exact likeness of the bride's Chihuahua. All of this embodies what creativity looks like.

Or does it?

Like everything else in life, creativity has a stereotype. Let's bust that stereotype right now.

Teachers don't generally identify themselves as creative professionals, at least not in the way that designers, artists, writers, architects, filmmakers, and even florists do. People with a strong desire to create something out of nothing don't typically choose education for their life's work. Sure, we know that kids have active imaginations and respond well to creative play. But in this era of standardized testing and scripted curriculums, teachers often feel limited as to what they can do in the classroom. Some educators think of creativity in terms of "arts and crafts" and decide creativity is not in the cards for them because they teach science or history rather than art or music. We're here to tell you that no matter what subject or grade you teach, you can make your classroom a vibrant, creative space—and that there are important reasons to do so.

We want you to throw out every notion you currently hold about what creativity looks like or how it functions. We ask that you banish from your brain all comparisons between yourself and iconic geniuses in the arts and sciences. Forget Mozart, Hemingway, Tesla, Spielberg, and Jobs.

In this book we're going to give you a new definition of creativity *as it applies to teaching.* We're going to show you that creativity can become your mindset in the classroom, whether or not you're "craftsy," and that you can tap into your own inner well of inspiration (Yes, you have one!) to motivate your students and allow them to reach their full potential because they are engaged with learning.

We've been on our own creative journeys for the better part of a decade now, and we're excited to share our own experiences with you as well as invite you to join us on this path and undergo your own creative breakthrough. Now at this point, you may be wondering why you even *need* a creative breakthrough. The answer is simple: *Because in the game of life, children have no control over the hand they are dealt. You, as a teacher, are the wild card that can make a difference in your students' lives.* And you can't do that if your classroom is static and uninspiring.

Before your start your own journey, we'll back up a bit and tell you a little about where we've been.

Our Own Path

Within the field of education, we're a bit of a novelty: a married couple teaching and working together at the same school, first at Pendleton Elementary in South Carolina and currently at the famed Ron Clark Academy in Atlanta. We're partners not only in life, but in a common career path with a shared goal of improving education through a focus on student engagement. When we first met, we were

Hope and Wade have almost as much fun as their students during the Jurassic Park science lesson.

young teachers just out of university. Right away, we found something we had in common: Both of us had grown up with a special creative interest and were now experimenting with bringing that authentic part of us into the classroom in ways that felt natural. These interests (for Wade it was music, and for Hope it was crafts) became anchors for teaching reading and math skills in innovative ways. By drawing on them, we were able to create lessons that our students were absorbed with and persisted at despite a high level of academic challenge. Best of all, our students exhibited joy and delight when they accomplished the work.

In this way we learned early on that it's not just the content but the delivery method that matters. Today, we go all out to find ways to implement our wildest ideas—because we've learned that creativity is the key to engagement, and engagement is the magic pixie dust that makes kids want to come to school.

And yes, it's true that "student engagement" can sometimes seem like a hollow buzzword. Yet increasingly it is seen as a much-needed outcome of K–12 educational reforms in an era when the U.S. college dropout rate for first-time students at a four-year university is hovering around fifty percent. Even when our students are earning the grades and test scores to get into college, they aren't engaged or committed enough to stay there for four years because they never became lifelong learners.

We believe student engagement and a love of learning are lacking in so many classrooms because too many teachers don't truly understand what engagement is or what it looks like. Most of us were taught to focus on standards and assessments. But let's face it: When teachers focus *only* on standards and assessments, they burn out quickly. Between thirty and forty percent leave the profession entirely within their first five years for a variety of reasons. Among those who stick it out, a whopping sixty-two percent say they spend too much time preparing students for state-mandated tests, while eighty-one percent say the students themselves spend too much time taking state- or district-mandated tests.

We believe teachers become frustrated and burned out because this focus on standards and assessments doesn't fulfill them or make them feel effective. They don't see excitement or growth or a love of learning in their classroom—because kids don't care about standardized testing. *Kids care about the things they enjoy.* They gravitate toward stuff that sparks their natural curiosity. They focus their attention on anything that awakens their sense of wonder and awe. Tapping into this kid-centered energy is crucial. We've seen it over and over again: When teachers use creative instruction methods, test scores naturally rise. It's a different mindset about "teaching to the test," and we see it like this: As educators, our job should be to make our children excited to come to class. That's why "set the stage to engage" has become our mantra for teaching.

We know from experience, however, that not everyone has the tools or the mindset to "set the stage." And that's where the idea of a creative breakthrough comes in.

Flexing the Creative Muscle

Remember, for our purposes we're redefining creativity as it applies to teaching.

Even if you've never painted a portrait or written a poem, your creative breakthrough is just ahead. Inspiration is all around you. We'll show you how to draw on your authentic self—your past experiences, personality quirks, interests, hobbies, and strengths—to deliver your content in more engaging ways. What if you're an athlete? What if you're good at building things? What if you're a cook or a gardener? What if you research your family tree or go to antique car shows? Whatever your special thing is, you can use it to make your content come to life. Too many teachers are hesitant to do that because they don't know how. We're going to show you how.

Our dream is for teachers from K–12 (Perhaps even beyond!) to independently and intentionally start flexing and strengthening their creative muscle. We want you to create not just lessons, but learning *experiences* and memorable moments for your students, which is how we define engagement. The benefits of student engagement speak for themselves: Your students will actually want to come to school, and you'll enjoy increased job satisfaction and professional growth. If you've lost some of your passion for teaching, we're going to help you find it again by incorporating your interests and personal passions into the content you teach.

We're not telling you to be just like us—just the opposite! We're writing this book together, as a couple, to show you that different people can be on very different paths yet still be working toward the same goal. We come from very different backgrounds and have different interests. In some ways, we're total opposites. We've evolved as educators in different ways and have had creative breakthroughs that reflect who we are as individuals, not as a couple.

Your path and your creative breakthrough is all about *you* and what makes you tick; it's not about anyone else. And it's definitely not about comparing your own brand of creativity to anyone else's. There's a good reason that comparison is said to be the thief of joy and the enemy of authenticity. Your creativity will look very different from Hope King's creativity, just as Hope's creativity is very different from Wade King's creativity. You don't have to mimic anyone's style or attempt to duplicate anyone else's level of success. Your path is to find your own creative style.

Along the way there will be obstacles. That's a given. Without the roadblocks, it wouldn't be a journey. If becoming a more creative teacher were easy, everyone would be on top of it, and no one would care about a book like this. We started giving our speeches and workshops because we were being asked repeatedly *How do you come up with your ideas?* and *How are you so creative?* This book is a way to answer those questions. It's a way to walk you through the steps that will lead you to your own creative breakthrough.

We've aimed for a book that is not just a pep talk but more like a "how-to" guide that anyone can implement. The book is structured into three parts:

- Part One briefly explains some of our key concepts and forms the foundation for your breakthrough.

- Part Two provides simple, straightforward steps that build on each other as you move toward a more creative mindset. We say "simple" because they're not rocket science and don't require huge amounts of time or money. What they *do* require is your willingness to get uncomfortable, to challenge yourself, to make changes, and to try something new. You may want to read the whole section to the end before going back and actively working through each step. It's up to you.

- Part Three is a toolbox of instructional strategies that have worked for us. They're not lesson plans, but rather frameworks you can plug your own ideas into. Some of them won't be right for you. Others will take a bit of practice, risk-taking, and trial and error. The idea is that everyone has to start somewhere, and we're going to give you that "somewhere" within these pages.

Throughout the book, we'll often be writing as a couple with one unified voice. Occasionally, however, we'll offer our individual voices where our experiences differ. By the end of the book, you'll have concrete ways to exercise your creative muscle. You'll be on the way to your creative breakthrough!

READY? Let's get started!

PART I
Wild Card

The cards always look different when it's your turn to play them; loaded with subtly different possibilities.

—Alastair Reynolds,
Revelation Space

We're using the metaphor of a *wild card* in two different ways here, linking both to teachers and to student engagement. The first, as we said in the Introduction, is the idea that teachers are persons of uncertain influence in their students' lives. The second is the more slangy use of wild card to describe a person who is unpredictable, full of surprises, or a little bit wacky. And that leads us back to the idea of creativity.

The dictionary defines creativity as *the ability to transcend traditional ideas, rules, patterns, or relationships and to create meaningful new ideas, forms, methods, interpretations, etc.* We personally believe that every teacher in the world has this ability—including you! You can transcend that standardized curriculum you're stuck with. You can build more inspired relationships with your students. And you can create meaningful new ways to deliver content. Right this minute, start believing that you have this ability within you! As bestselling author Elizabeth Gilbert puts it, "The universe buries strange jewels within us all and then stands back to see if we can find them." That's what your creative breakthrough is all about—tapping into the inner resources you may not have known you had.

Before you start on the steps toward a creative breakthrough in Part II, open your mind to the idea that you really can grow and evolve. You're probably familiar with the concepts of *fixed mindset* and *growth mindset* as they relate to education. People with a fixed mindset believe intelligence is a static trait that was predetermined at birth, while those with a growth mindset believe they can grow their intellect. It's the same with creativity. You can either tell yourself you were born without it, or you can choose to actively develop it. We urge you to develop a growth mindset regarding your potential for creativity. Before you can have a creative breakthrough, you must have faith it is possible. This section will help you become a believer.

CHAPTER ONE
The Game of Life

*Each player must accept the cards life deals
him or her; but once they are in hand, he or
she alone must decide how to play the cards
in order to win the game.*

—Voltaire

A while back, we read an essay that stuck with us. The author was reflecting on how so much in life depends on the luck of the draw. His idea was that real life is not at all like the game of *Monopoly*, where all players start on the same square with equal resources and earn another $200 every time they circle back to GO. It's more like poker, where players receive a randomly dealt hand of cards that may be strong or weak—or somewhere in between, so that anything can happen, depending on luck, strategy, and the cards held by other players. That concept was our starting point for the *wild card* metaphor.

Think about it: Children don't have control over their daily lives and the dynamics of "nature" and "nurture" that shape their early experiences. They are dealt a hand that includes their parents—supportive, neglectful, indulgent, or absent—and their socioeconomic status. The luck of the draw determines the neighborhoods they live in and the schools they attend. A roll of the genetic dice shapes the characteristics and personality traits that affect learning: gender, intelligence, attention span, resiliency, self-discipline, and talents.

Very few kids, even those with involved parents and strong socioeconomic resources, have been dealt the real-life equivalent of a full house or a royal flush. Children who are left holding the weakest possible hands—which might include anything from an unstable home environment to a learning disability—don't have the option to fold their cards and sit out the round until their odds improve. They have no choice but to play the hands they're dealt. Essentially, childhood is one randomly dealt hand that can influence everything else in life.

WADE: I had a rough childhood. My parents divorced soon after I was born and I never knew my dad. My mom made some bad choices with the men she dated and, as a result, I was horribly abused as a preschooler. People think young children don't form lasting memories, but I know otherwise because I remember everything that was done to me during those years. Finally, my grandmother and her husband took me into their home. When I was about four, we all traveled to Athens, Greece, a place my grandma had always wanted to see. I can still close my eyes and recall the sights and sounds. I remember the goats grazing on the green hills and the tall columns of the Parthenon. I remember the dense, crusty bread. I loved it there, and it's the reason ancient civilization is my favorite content to teach today. The fact that I have these memories reinforces for me that memorable experiences—good or bad—really do stick with kids forever.

We stayed in Greece for about eleven months. Now, that's a long time for a vacation, and later it became clear why we had spent so much time there. The trip had been my grand-mother's last wish. She had cancer and died shortly after we returned home. I went to live with an uncle and aunt then. It was my third home and family, and I was only five. For a few years I had a pretty normal childhood, including holidays, family vacations, a cousin who was like a sister to me, and all that good stuff. But that wasn't meant to be, either.

My aunt and uncle divorced when I was around eleven—old enough to feel heartbroken over losing the family I loved and a stable home environment. I desperately wanted to stay with my aunt and cousin, and I was able to for a year. Then I was shuffled off again to live with my uncle in a condo on the beach. It was a decent home until went through a difficult

Young Wade at the beach shortly after going to live with his grandmother.

time. He sold everything our family had owned, and by the time I was in eighth grade I was basically homeless in South Carolina. I resorted to sleeping in the park when my friends' doors were locked or they weren't home. When my asthma got bad, I stole inhalers from Revco.

At that point, school was the only consistent thing I'd ever known in my life. I wasn't a great student, and I didn't care much about learning. I went to school every day because I didn't have any place else to go. I needed teachers to push me, and I'm grateful now that they did. I'm grateful I fell into good friendships as well. When I was in tenth grade, a friend invited me to a Bible study group, and that was a turning point. I realized I couldn't have gotten to where I was without the two constants in my life: teachers and Jesus. I knew I couldn't become Jesus, so it was then I decided I was going to be a teacher. I was still a struggling student—I think I took algebra three or four times before I passed—but I'd found my purpose in life.

Wade's friends secretly raised money to pay his way for the class trip to New York City.

Young Hope and her father, Warren, exploring caves in the Midwest

HOPE: I have wonderful memories of an idyllic childhood in rural South Carolina. My family was close, and we belonged to a very close-knit church community. My brother and I were practically raised in the church; we were there any time the doors were open. My mom and dad were involved with the youth ministry program, and I loved it when my dad was in charge of locking up the church because it meant I got to stay late and play with my friends.

My mom left an accounting job to stay home with us while we were little. She brought tremendous creativity to everything she did. She taught me all kinds of hands-on crafting skills and even homeschooled me during the years I was in fifth and sixth grade. She was by far the toughest teacher I ever had!

I went to public school from seventh grade on so I could participate in the athletic programs. I had started running races with my dad when I was five years old. In fact, I took first place and received a medal for my very first one-mile race ever. I think that was the beginning of my competitive streak. My dad would ask if I wanted to enter this race or that race, and the first thing out of my mouth would be, "Is there a big trophy?" And I'd usually win. Over the years I ran track, played basketball, and dabbled in just about every sport you can imagine. My dad was always one of the coaches, and he was tough; he made me work really hard. At the time, I was confused as to why he seemed to push me harder than anyone else on the team, but I completely understand it now—he believed in me even more than I believed in myself. He was helping me discover my full potential.

My parents never missed a sporting or school event I participated in. They supported me and shaped me to have a strong backbone. They never made excuses for me or coddled me, so the work ethic came early to me. I was confident enough to go after the things I wanted and to make my own opportunities. I owe a lot to my parents. As a child, you never quite grasp that concept of "you'll thank me later." But now? Yep. I get it.

Every child's metaphorical hand includes one very important wild card—a person whose influence is unpredictable and whose qualities are uncertain. That person is you. As a teacher, *you* are the wild card. Children who've been dealt a strong hand in the game of life might flourish no matter who their teachers are. Others depend on that wild card to change the game. Will you be the teacher who finds a way to inspire, engage, and uplift every child? Or will you fail those children who need you the most by stifling their love of learning and sending them on to an uneasy future? Remember, a wild card can go either way. You can shape either lifelong learners or students who feel like learning is a chore rather than an opportunity.

Creativity Is a Personal Brand

We began our teaching careers in elementary school education in a rural district faced with many challenges. Pendleton Elementary, where we taught, had the lowest test scores in the district. The state intervened and brought us into the South Carolina TAP program (SC TAP), otherwise known as the System for Teacher and Student Advancement. In an effort to standardize the quality of instruction across the state, the school board handed all of us a scripted curriculum for every subject we taught. We had no choice but to follow the script.

Now, it's easy to see how a scripted lesson could be the enemy of creativity. But let's imagine a room full of actors auditioning for a part, all reading the same scripted lines out loud. It doesn't matter if they're amateur thespians or Hollywood's finest. The point is, they'll all draw on their own personal brand of dramatic flair to choose voice inflections, facial expressions, and hand gestures while delivering those lines. Each actor's audition will be different. Some will shine. Some will deliver lines that fall flat. It's the same for teachers. You have to decide how you will breathe life into your curriculum, regardless of what it is. If a scripted curriculum is part of the hand you've been dealt as a teacher, you'll need a good game strategy.

For us, the strategy was to teach the scripted curriculum as required, but to do it quickly and then take it to the next level—by

Lucky's Punctuation Patty-O was one of Hope's first room transformations.

teaching supplemental material above grade level and including activities that engaged our students. This was when we discovered we could create magic by using our hobbies and interests in the classroom. Wade drew on his athletic background to come up with competitive games that made math more engaging. He brought his electric guitar to school and began writing content-heavy song lyrics that helped kids remember vocabulary and terminology. Hope used her skill at crafting to develop the instructional strategy she eventually became well known for: the room transformation. Her early efforts were quite simple, such as draping green plastic tablecloths over desks and hanging shamrock cutouts on the wall to transport the kids to "Lucky's Punctuation Patty-O." The idea was to create an environment that would set the mood for and support the content Hope was teaching. (It worked so well that her room transformations grew more and more elaborate over time, pulling in music, sound effects, props, and even costumes.)

We were just beginning to flex our creative muscle, yet our test scores quickly reflected our efforts. At one point, Wade's students were testing at the 94th percentile, and the majority (96 percent) of Hope's students scored as having met or exceeded expectations on the state's standardized test. Keep in mind that most of our students were struggling when they arrived. Eighty percent of them were testing between the first and thirty-ninth percentile on MAP standardized testing.

In short, our winning strategy was to boost student engagement by delivering our content creatively, despite the scripted curriculum. This can be your strategy too—but you'll be employing your own personal brand of creativity, not mimicking ours.

Creativity Is a Mindset

In 2009 our administrator at Pendleton Elementary sent every teacher in the school for professional development at the Ron Clark Academy (RCA) in Georgia. In all honesty, we didn't think, at first, that the teaching techniques at a middle school would cross over into our first- and third-grade classrooms.

Yet something changed for us and for Pendleton Elementary after that trip.

RCA is a vibrant place with a striking décor and high-energy teachers. It's a place where creativity is encouraged, and educators are given the opportunity to stretch and evolve into the best versions of themselves. The more we saw, the more inspired we became. We knew we couldn't duplicate the electric-blue slide and the "secret" passageways—but we also realized that when it comes right down to it, kids are just kids. Our students are the heart of it all, with or without a two-story slide. We returned to Pendleton and started implementing the ideas we'd gotten from the RCA experience, adapting them as necessary to fit our younger kids. We even established the "house system" that RCA uses to create joy, camaraderie, and close connections between children at different grade levels. And we figured out a way to do it without a giant spinning jackpot wheel to sort the kids into houses, because props like that are just the icing on the cake—and we were still baking our cake.

Our visit to RCA affirmed for us that we were on the right path. It also made us realize we were only taking baby steps, and we knew we could do more. So we continued to challenge our students and set high expectations. We strengthened our commitment to seeing the whole child, rather than making excuses for kids based on their home lives or family incomes or attention deficits. And then we took a crucial giant leap to move our creative efforts to the next level: We mustered up the grit to translate our wildest ideas into action. We'd had a lot of lessons and concepts floating around in our heads but had been afraid to put effort into something that might flop horribly in the classroom. Our RCA visit inspired us to get past this fear of failure and to take risks. If you never get to visit RCA (although we hope you do), we can tell you that the single most important thing we learned there is this: *The educators at RCA are masters of creating the unexpected.* By cultivating the ability to startle and surprise students, teachers—including you—can become a "wild card" in yet another sense by being so unpredictable that students never know what's in store for them when they get to class.

Once we started stretching ourselves and making the effort to shake up our students with something—anything—out of the ordinary, everything was transformed. At first it didn't take much to surprise our kids because, to them, school was static and boring. We could show up to class in a wacky costume, lay artificial turf on the classroom floor, rock out on an electric guitar, or have the kids write their answers on Frisbees instead of paper. Suddenly, we had their attention! As we experimented with creative ways to bring our lessons to life, we worried less about looking foolish or failing. As a result, we were greeted every day with the gleeful anticipation of children who looked forward to coming to school—and who finished their current grade eager to start the next grade level.

Creativity Drives Engagement

One of our Pendleton Elementary students—we'll call her Kaylie—had not been dealt a winning hand in life. We could see the untapped brilliance in her. Kaylie had so much potential, but her home life was a disaster. She didn't always show up for school in clean clothes or with her hair brushed. She couldn't always concentrate in class because sometimes she was hungry, sleepy, or simply bored. We'll never forget the day she arrived at school with a soaking wet book bag. Its contents, including books Hope had lent her, were ruined and beyond saving. Kaylie had slept in the cab of a pickup truck the previous night, with her book bag in the truck bed, and it had rained hard.

We would look at students like Kaylie and think, *I know the state says I should do it a certain way, but I need to go above and beyond that.* After we started on our creative paths, Kaylie was the student in whom we saw the most dramatic change. When Wade met the bus in the morning, Kaylie would leap off the bottom step and run up to him. "Mr. King, Mr. King, tell me what Ms. King's doing today," she would beg. "Does she have a new song? Is she wearing a costume? What are we gonna learn?"

That is how every single child should feel every single day. As a teacher, you have the power to create this eagerness to come to school. When your students can't wait to see what you'll do next, you become the wild card that just might change the game for them. You become the wild card that potentially trumps the weaker cards in the metaphorical hand they've been dealt. Who, as a teacher, wouldn't want to wield this power?

Flash forward a few years, and we've now spent nearly a decade furthering our interest in creative instruction methods. We've discovered what works consistently. Every day we learn a bit more about what doesn't work, and why. Along the way we've shared our most successful ideas with other teachers through social media platforms, live video presentations, speeches, workshops, and our blog, *Elementary Shenanigans*. This book is the next step in our own creative evolution and our mission to promote student engagement. We want you to become that *Wild Card* teacher who gives each child a winning hand in the game of life.

CHAPTER TWO

The Deck Is *Not* Stacked Against You

Everything is easier said than done.
Don't give yourself that excuse.

—Sue Fitzmaurice,
Purpose

At our conferences and workshops, we often hear teachers talk about their frustrations. They feel as if they're stranded on an uncharted island, trying to do things by themselves with limited resources. They struggle to build a hut out of palm fronds, when they really want concrete and bricks to build a solid house on a strong foundation. They wade in up to their necks, and before they know it they're in over their heads and feel like they're drowning. We often felt like that, and maybe you feel this way even now. If so, please rescue yourself from that island before this feeling becomes a death spiral. We've seen it play out this way too many times. As teachers get tired of putting forth effort that doesn't bring results, they desperately want permission to stop trying so hard, so they find plenty of excuses for why their students are not more engaged.

The trouble is, it's easy for excuse-making to become a habit. Every less-than-ideal factor can become another reason why your students aren't achieving more—and why you can't do anything to change that. It happens all the time, as teachers convince themselves they've been dealt a bad hand, year after year. The list of excuses is pretty predictable: no funding, no parental involvement, Title I, a high percentage of ESL students, unsupportive administrators, standardized testing, scripted curriculums, crowded classrooms, never enough time.

These factors are real, and you have to deal with them. We get it; that's the environment we came from too. We could have made any of those excuses for ourselves or used them as reasons to give up. (And believe us, some days we wanted to!) We faced tremendous challenges, many of them stemming from constant transitions in leadership. Pendleton Elementary went through four administrators in six years, and with every new admin came a new set of expectations. Between the state's scripted curriculum and Common Core, we felt the effects of "curriculum whiplash" because we weren't sticking with anything long enough to understand how well—or *if*—it worked. On top of everything else, Pendleton had most of the district's special-education students, and over 80 percent of our kids qualified for free or reduced lunch programs. On Fridays, our school nurse would pack food bags for those kids who might not otherwise eat again until Monday. We even knew of elementary students who were setting their own alarms for 6:00 a.m. and walking themselves to the bus stop, then walking home to an empty house every afternoon. During Hope's first year at Pendleton, she had six students with incarcerated dads and only two with both biological parents living in the home. Since we were a choice district, the most involved parents in the surrounding neighborhood chose not to send their kids to our school.

It's no wonder the Pendleton teachers were exhausted and in danger of burning out, even though many of them were phenomenal educators. We were all facing tremendous challenges, pouring so much of ourselves into those kids, and still the state looked at our standardized test scores and officially recognized us as failures. Being judged so harshly despite our efforts made it hard to feel motivated at times. It was downright discouraging. And it certainly made the Pendleton teachers hesitant to try new things when there was no guarantee a new approach would produce the test scores the state was looking for.

On the other hand, the district as a whole was one of the best in the state—so many of the Pendleton teachers had the heart and the desire to turn Pendleton Elementary around too. Many of us chose not to believe the deck was stacked against us, including the administrator who sent every teacher in the school for professional development at the Ron Clark Academy.

Instead of throwing up our hands and letting our challenges become excuses for why we couldn't do better as educators, we both looked for ways to get over those hurdles. Finding creative ways to deliver our content was key. As we channeled our creative energy into boosting engagement, and as creativity became part of our personal brands, other teachers began paying attention. That's when we first started hearing, "How do you do it?"

For us, the journey began with the fact that we truly believed in those kids. It wasn't something we were just saying—we meant it, and that belief drove our "no excuses" mindset. We chose not to see those kids as the sum of their clothes, houses, and parents' incomes. Instead, we saw them as individuals with untapped potential we could unlock. We cared about their futures, and we didn't waste our days shaking our heads over their present struggles.

Once we were able to boost student engagement, the test scores and attendance records rose as well—*which meant the abilities or socioeconomic status of our kids were never the "excuse" for their performance.*

Remember, wealthy districts also have issues that teachers complain about: unmotivated kids who've had everything handed to them, helicopter parents, and a pervasive sense of entitlement. It could be just as easy to turn these things into excuses for student performance or why you can't engage your students. You have to teach standards; that's a given. But standards don't determine how you *deliver* the content—and it's your delivery method that drives engagement. As we'll show you, there are ways to be creative within the framework of any educational system. No matter what you face in your own classroom, school, or district, the deck is not stacked against you. When you are confronted with challenges, setbacks, or students who are hard to reach, don't allow those things to serve as excuses. Every year you'll have a new set of challenges and a different group of students. This will be true for your entire career, so you have to start every year with a new vision. It's a new hand of cards. How will you play it?

CHAPTER THREE
Don't Listen to the Joker

*Our doubts are traitors, and make us lose the
good we oft might win, by fearing to attempt.*

—William Shakespeare,
Measure for Measure

We hope by now your mind is open to change and you're thinking about how you will play your hand. If you've adopted a growth mindset, you are primed for your creative breakthrough. You're ready to take small steps outside your comfort zone because inertia no longer has a hold on you. Those tired, old excuses have revealed themselves as lies, and they can't stop you now.

What *will* stop you dead in your tracks, however, is the Joker—if you let him.

The Joker is the internal dialogue of doubt, that voice inside your head that tells you nothing is good enough. The Joker scoffs at your early efforts and warns you that a failure is just around the bend. When something doesn't go as planned, the Joker is right there ready to shame you. When you succeed at something, the Joker shrugs and tells you it was just a one-time fluke. Since the Joker knows you will no longer use external factors as excuses to give up, he will pit you against yourself. He will try to turn you into your own roadblock.

Don't listen to the Joker when he tells you...

- *You'll never pull that off.*
- *You may think you pulled that off, but it was mediocre at best.*
- *You'll look stupid.*
- *Your students will laugh at you.*
- *You're too old to make a change.*
- *You don't have a creative bone in your body.*
- *That other teacher is just so good; you can't compete with that.*

Do you see what the Joker is doing? He's finding the seeds of things that exist in all of us—doubt, self-consciousness, perfectionism, jealousy, negative comparisons, fear—and trying to make them sprout and grow. Don't let your mind be fertile ground for these thorny weeds.

When you're on the creative path, the number one thing the Joker will try to convince you of is this: *That idea is not original. It has been done many times before. You did not create that.*

Well, there aren't very many original ideas in education. And it doesn't matter. If your students find your lessons fresh and new to them, they will be engaged. Also keep in mind that all artists are links in a chain of influence. Prince was influenced by James Brown and Stevie Wonder. If you start with a concept you borrowed from another source, and you adapt it and pour your own self into it, you'll be better than original—you'll be authentic, just like Prince.

Change the Dialogue

Both of us have moments when confidence is in short supply. When we give workshops and presentations, we're often speaking to teachers who have more years of teaching experience than we have. It can give us a bad case of the jitters. Often, just before a talk, the Joker whispers to us that every person in that audience is sitting there passing judgment on us, thinking, *Well, what do they know?* Self-doubt wiggles in and we find ourselves doubting our own credibility, wondering if we even deserve to be teaching at the Ron Clark Academy at this stage in our careers, because at the time we were hired, there were a lot of very seasoned teachers at the school.

At times like this, we talk back to the Joker. We inform him that we don't have to be perfect to speak about what we've experienced so far. We remind him that we've spent ten years working on student engagement and creativity in the classroom and we have a good understanding of what works. When the Joker tries to fill us with stage fright, we overcome it by changing our internal dialogue, pulling up thoughts that are positive and realistic for us at that moment in time. You can use a similar strategy.

Every now and then, however, the Joker gets the better of us—like the time we were on our way to give a talk in Nevada, and Hope had a panic attack on the plane, thinking about the size of the audience at that event. If there had been a way to turn the plane around, she would have done that. She was convinced she couldn't pull off a ninety-minute talk, and the doubts continued even after the speech began.

You may have similar moments when you're too tired or discouraged to have a debate with the Joker. Maybe those moments even turn into days or weeks. That's okay. We can assure you those times will pass. Just because the Joker fooled you once doesn't mean you have to give up completely. You can get back on your creative path, resume your efforts, and offer a confident rebuttal to the Joker the next time he rears his head.

Shrug Off Setbacks

As you try out new strategies in the classroom, you'll have a few flops and blunders. It's inevitable. And of course, the Joker will try to use your misadventures against you. He'll call them failures because he is hoping to push you back into a fixed mindset. He wants you to fall so hard for the line that you cannot be creative that you never get back up again.

The truth is, your bloopers don't mean you're failing. They're a sign that you're stretching and growing and exploring the possibilities. The old cliché is true: People often have to learn through their mistakes so they can do it better the next time. Here's an example: Wade once stepped outside his comfort zone to do an elaborate room transformation to set the stage for a two-day lesson about the United Nations. The theme was Power Rangers, and Wade spent two weeks building and painting his versions of the Command Center and Power Chambers in our garage. Then came time to set it all up in his classroom. But he'd never done this before. So instead of tacking everything securely, he hung all the backdrops and props with flimsy cellophane tape the night before—and everything was lying on the floor in heaps when he arrived on the big day, just five minutes before school started.

The Joker loved it. *See? You can't pull off anything that elaborate. You should stick to what you know.*

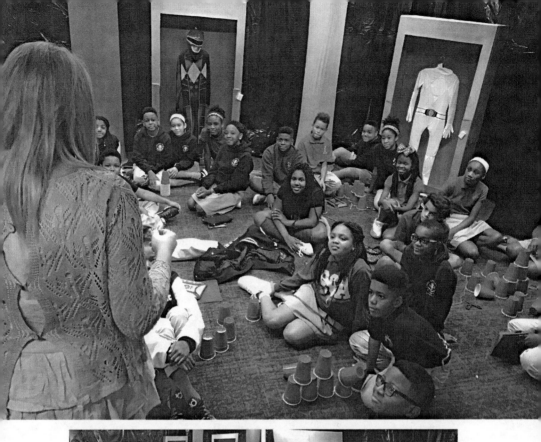

With the Joker taunting him like that, Wade was ready to give up and hold class in a different room. However, he had pulled a lot of strings to arrange a surprise for the students: The actor who originally played the character of the Green Ranger, Jason David Frank, was making an appearance at our school that day. Wade was stuck. He could not give in to the Joker. The show had to go on—despite the fact the props continued to fall throughout the lesson.

Rookie mistakes lead to growth and mastery.

What the Joker won't tell you is that these rookie mistakes lead to growth and mastery. As author Julia Cameron points out in *The Artist's Way,* "In order to do something well, we must first be willing to do it badly." If you limit yourself to only doing the things you know you're good at, you cannot have a creative breakthrough.

There are other times we've had spectacular setbacks, moments when we wanted to be absolutely killing it but ended up feeling like we'd made fools of ourselves. One year on Parents Day, Hope taught a language arts class dressed as a flapper, complete with a bobbed wig and a jazzy dress. She was doing her thing with forty parents observing from the back of the room when a young student up-front began making soft hissing sounds and gesturing to get her attention. Hope just kept teaching, as the student's eyes grew bigger and the gestures grew more frantic. Then Hope suddenly realized she was feeling a draft … and we'll just let it go at that.

The Joker enjoyed himself immensely that day. *Ha ha! You not only looked foolish—you did it in front of all those moms and dads!*

You, too, will have times when your plan (or your costume!) falls apart, comes undone, or exposes you to embarrassment. With practice, you can learn to ignore the Joker's wisecracks and talk back to him when he is disparaging you. Set the Joker straight. Get in his face. Tell him firmly that you're on a creative path and will not be sidetracked. Tell him you don't mind a few setbacks for the sake of growth. Tell him this time around, you're playing your hand without a Joker.

PART II

Creative Breakthrough

Just release yourself from the anxiety and burden that might be associated with the word 'creativity,' because you've fallen for the myth that it only belongs to the special, the tormented, and the professional.

—Elizabeth Gilbert,
Big Magic

To know your limits is a state of self-delusion.

—Bill Purdin

When we first met Rebecca, she was firmly settled into middle age and had been teaching fifth grade for many years in the same public school. She had adjusted to Common Core and had built up a large stockpile of classroom supplies and teaching materials over the years. It was a somewhat comfortable existence, because she knew her lesson plans by heart. Yet at the same time, Rebecca was getting tired of the repetition. She was experiencing a bit of burnout and was at the point where her professional plateau could easily become a dangerous sinkhole. Let's face it, many teachers in a similar circumstance are just marking time and coasting toward the finish line of retirement.

Then Rebecca came to observe our classes and our teaching methods—and things began to change. She felt a little spark of inspiration and, to her credit, she acted on it. One of the things that really struck her at our school was how the students and teachers ate lunch together, talking and laughing. So Rebecca took a deep breath and asked a group of her fifth-graders if she could share their lunch table. To her surprise, the kids were so excited by this small gesture that they almost forgot to eat! That first day they all talked about their pets, and Rebecca learned how much compassion and empathy her students had for animals.

This positive response encouraged Rebecca to keep going. She sat with a different group of kids every day for a month, getting to know them as people and learning about their interests outside of school. At first Rebecca assumed she'd burn out quickly with no real break at lunchtime. Instead, she felt energized and inspired by the new bonds she was forming and the new insights she had about the kids as individuals.

Rebecca's next step outside her comfort zone was to trade her usual worksheets for a more interactive learning approach. While teaching fractions and decimals, she made up a series of hand and arm gestures for each related concept. She spent a few minutes at the beginning of class demonstrating each one, and then had her students bring a static worksheet to life as they went through the problems together and solved each one with movement. This was Rebecca's turning point. When she saw her students completely absorbed with least common denominators and decimal conversions, their eyes locked on her hand motions, she knew she could never go back to her old ways of teaching. Soon Rebecca was figuring out ways to bring movement to all the "humdrum" topics.

As Rebecca worked at doing something different every week, she started to look forward to teaching in a way she hadn't for a long time. She enjoyed those moments when she had her students' full attention, and it reignited an old spark, reminding her of the days many years earlier when she had performed in community theater. Inspired, she took the plunge and showed up to class in a colonial costume one day, speaking to her students as if she were a historical figure. She was teaching the same Common Core material about colonial America as always, yet her students were truly engaged. It was as if she'd stepped out of a time machine. The kids completely bought into her role-play. They listened and asked questions—and they learned.

Over time, Rebecca took many more baby steps toward gradually changing her teaching style and her classroom. She is now one of the top-performing teachers at her school.

A creative breakthrough like Rebecca's doesn't happen overnight. We usually think of it as a two-year process. So often, the things that work with one class don't work as well the following year with a different group of kids, so you learn how to build on your earlier efforts. Creative change is all about experimentation and personal transformation, and that can make it an uneasy—but rewarding—process.

We've learned that when we're comfortable, we're no longer growing or improving. We both weathered a period of tremendous discomfort when we first moved to Atlanta. For us, RCA was the perfect opportunity—but it was also the perfect storm. At Pendleton we'd grown to be confident, solid teachers. Now we were in a place where everyone else was confident and successful, and *we* were the new kids on the block. We had to prove ourselves, but the things that had worked well for us in elementary school often fell flat in middle school. We found that RCA had extremely rigorous expectations. To teach those expectations, we had to learn them—and the students knew them better than we did. Talk about a confidence buster! At times, we completely doubted our abilities. We weren't sure we were cut out for this new environment. To top it all off, there were hundreds of other educators coming in to observe the teaching methods at RCA, so we were sweating under the spotlight.

For a time, we struggled. Wade lost sight of his own talents and found himself trying to emulate other teachers. His students often had to explain school procedures to him. He was teaching in the library and missed having his own space. Hope struggled to find her creative voice. She was also sharing a classroom with another teacher. On one of the worst days of her career, Hope had her students working on a group assignment when Ron Clark walked into the room to find a child hanging from the rafters like a monkey—the building is an old warehouse and the exposed posts and beams seemed like a jungle gym to Justin. Now, if you know Hope, you know she has high expectations when it comes to behavior. Nothing like this had ever happened to her before. NOT EVER. But on this day, to top it all off, her new admin now had a reason to doubt her classroom-management skills.

And of course, when it rains it pours—literally. Our brand-new condo leaked everywhere, so after those tough days at school, we came home to a place that was completely covered in plastic sheeting and almost uninhabitable. We struggled to keep our professional wardrobes dry and neat looking. We ate every meal in the bedroom. Hope heated spaghetti in the bathtub with warm water. This went on for two months. Without a safe haven in which to unwind after work, our stress levels rose even higher.

It was like we were first-year teachers all over again, trying to figure it out—both life and work—and get adjusted. And we did adjust. But we also learned that to live creatively means you always have to push the margins a little. You can't fall into the mindset that you've reached the top and no longer need to innovate. Life isn't supposed to be about doing the same thing over and over again. From that year of discomfort came tremendous growth.

Writing this book also required us to step outside our comfort zone. In fact, it's the hardest thing we've ever done. We've mostly come to terms with the stage fright we feel from public speaking, but this project introduced us to the concept of "page fright" as we started to put our thoughts on paper. We had to come up with the confidence to get started and the motivation to keep going. We had a few false starts, and we did a lot of backtracking. We had to stretch ourselves beyond what felt safe, comfortable, routine—*and what we knew for sure we were good at.* And once again, the reward was tremendous professional growth.

We want you to shake things up a little too.

The next seven chapters are the steps we hope will lead you outside your comfort zone and toward a creative breakthrough. They're designed to build on each other. The early steps may be very easy for you—they'll likely become more challenging as you move through the chapters. You can either go through the book slowly, working through each step after finishing a chapter, or you can read through to the end before going back and actively working through each step. Another idea is to work through the book with a buddy. It could be another teacher at your school or a colleague who teaches a different grade or lives in another city. The idea is to find support and encouragement as you run ideas past each other, reflect on personal strengths and weaknesses, and learn from each other's victories and disappointments.

As long as our habit patterns are hidden backstage, they will remain unchanged. As soon as we bring them up onto the stage of our mind and shine the spotlight of awareness on them, they will inevitably change.

—Jan Chozen Bays

The first step toward change is awareness. The second step is acceptance.

—Nathaniel Branden

CHAPTER FOUR
Awareness

Evaluate where you are today and accept it so you can move forward.

It can be paralyzing to look at any goal or transition as one big scary task. You stand frozen in place, staring at the faraway finish line instead of taking the first baby step. But you have to start somewhere, so we're going to make it easy for you by providing a first step you can perform privately and in your own time. We recognize that this first step may be easy for you, or it may be painful. We want you to assess where you are right now and to be completely honest with yourself.

You may be a new teacher who is struggling to connect the dots between the educational theory you learned in college and the actual art of teaching in the classroom—maybe your instinct tells you something is missing, but you don't know what. You may be a mid-career teacher who feels confident about teaching, but you can also see that your students are often bored or unmotivated. You may love your job and feel like you're killing it based on the test scores you produce year after year. Or you may be a teacher who is facing many challenges, feeling the deck is stacked against you, running out of energy, and moving quickly toward complete professional burnout.

Your career stage and personal details don't matter in this process of self-assessment because everyone has room to stretch and grow. What matters is your honest answer to this question: Do your students *want* to be in your classroom, or do they merely *have* to be there?

Before you answer, let's make this question a little more personal. Think back to a time when you were told (not asked) to attend a professional development seminar that you just weren't interested in. You know, the seminar where you glanced at the clock pretty much every five minutes … and planned next month's lessons … and made a grocery list for a year's worth of dinners … and checked every social media app on your phone—twice. What percentage of yourself did you actually invest in bettering your craft and improving your teaching methods during that time?

When we ask this in our workshops, we rarely hear an answer over 50 percent—and the average is about 15 percent.

Let's apply this to your classroom. What if we polled your students and asked them if they genuinely want to be in school, or if they're only there because they have no choice? How would they answer? Is it likely they spend much of the day wishing they were somewhere—*anywhere*—else?

Let's face it, much like you in that long, boring meeting, many students are investing only a small percentage of their effort into learning. Yet teachers everywhere are scratching their heads, wondering why they aren't getting anywhere, why they reteach everything twice, why students don't retain knowledge.

Now imagine yourself in a professional development session that you really want to attend, one that is vibrant and fun and makes its point in ways that really speak to you as an educator. How much of yourself do you invest?

When we ask the question this way, our workshop participants often say 100 percent, and some even say 110 percent! So it's simple. If you want your students to give it their all, you have to make them *want* to be in your classroom. There is a reason fourth-graders don't skip around the playground singing about standards. (Can you even imagine that?) There's a reason tenth-graders don't text their friends *OMG, I love those educational assessments!* Standards and assessments are not the things that get kids excited about learning. Only you can do that. So we're going to say it again: If you currently feel powerless against the reality of a scripted curriculum and standardized testing, we're here to remind you that you, as a teacher, hold enormous power.

Hope once received an email from the parent of a student who was extremely sick but begging to attend school the next day. "Mrs.

King," the note read, "Robert cannot keep any food down at all. Can you please tell him it is okay for him to stay home until he's better?" *That* is the power teachers hold. No matter what kind of circumstances you teach under, you possess the ability to make your students excited about learning. You're like Dorothy with the ruby slippers. You have the power to create big magic; you just have to learn how to use it. (And it's a tiny bit more complicated than clicking your heels together, so stay with us as we explain!)

Assess, Accept, Act

If your honest evaluation tells you that your students are not engaged, or you're not getting results, or you don't feel fulfilled as an educator, then it's time to muster up the no-excuses mindset. You have to acknowledge the problem so you can realize you have greater potential to reach.

It can be hard to admit that something in your life has room for improvement because you're not living up to your full potential. Self-critique can sometimes feel a little too much like the downbeat dialogue of the Joker. If that starts to happen, try flipping the script. Make your internal dialogue all about empowering—rather than degrading—yourself. Try something like this:

> ***You know what? Something isn't working for me. What I've been doing, the way I've been teaching in the past is not as effective as I'd like it to be. I don't have it all together, and I've made mistakes. My choice is to grow and improve. I choose to focus on student engagement. I want to be a "wild card" and to have a creative breakthrough.***

Sometimes it's an outside comment or criticism that pushes you to reflection and self-evaluation. We've both found ourselves in a situation like this on more than one occasion. We get so many positive comments, but every so often we get one of *those* emails. You know the kind we mean: those critical comments that come from a parent and really sting. We've had a few that stung all the more because we honestly believed we'd been doing a good job. And—maybe you can relate to this—sometimes our kneejerk reaction has been to sit there and come up with excuses. *These parents just don't understand what I've done for their child. They haven't considered how much time I poured into this school or how much time I spent away from my family. They don't realize how hard it was to juggle teaching with some difficult personal problems this year. They have no idea how much effort I put into these lessons and learning experiences.*

Have you ever had a day when twenty-five great things happened but you let one bad thing ruin your day? We sometimes fall into that trap too. Despite the good feedback we get, we have occasionally focused on the feedback that was negative. We have even let ourselves get defensive and make excuses because it took away the sting and the feelings of failure. But we also realized we had a choice to make. We could sit there and wallow in our misery forever, or pause, reflect, and embrace the uncomfortable feelings. In the end, we often find we can't be angry about critical feedback because we can find some truth and value in the criticism. Once we admit to ourselves, *Okay, I can do better at that*, we're able to move past the meltdown and look ahead. We've even found that as soon as we accept where we are, it's natural to start coming up with ideas for ways to do it differently next year. No big deal, after all!

If you're feeling devastated or defensive over a negative evaluation, it's okay to have that meltdown. You just can't wallow in it forever; instead, let your dissatisfaction with those critical comments guide your process of self-assessment. Reflect on it, eat some cookies, call a friend, and move forward.

Acceptance is the true starting point for your breakthrough. It's hard to deal with criticism, regardless of the source. But the practice of self-assessment isn't meant to make you feel bad about yourself. *It's about taking an honest look at the results you're getting from your teaching methods.* If you can't get past this first step—assessment and acceptance—then this book can't help you recover your sense of purpose in the classroom or move on to make magic.

So how do you make sense of criticism and assess yourself as a teacher? One place to start is by reflecting on your WHY.

What's Your WHY?

No one chooses a career in education expecting to become a billionaire. As corny as it sounds, a lot of us started out with the idea we could change children's lives as a way to change the world. Then reality sets in. That's when it's time to re-evaluate why we're really doing what we do.

Every teacher has an individual WHY, a personal motive that changes over time. The two of us initially chose a career in education based on very different WHYs. Whenever we've stumbled or hit a rough patch in education, it's helped us to re-examine our sense of purpose and figure out what kind of WHY is currently driving us.

> **HOPE:** I always wanted to be a teacher. From the time I was four years old, I played school all the time. I never questioned my plan to become a teacher; I went after it with a laser focus. I graduated high school a year early, jumped into the education program at college, and never looked back. When I became an educator, I never thought, *What's my*

purpose? Why am I doing this? And that lack of purpose—not having a WHY—can become a huge weakness for people like me. When you really get into the trenches and face reality, education is not that imaginary classroom you taught as a child where everyone is perfect and your dolls just sit there quietly soaking up knowledge. During your first couple of years as a teacher, life might seem just fine because teaching is something new and fresh—you have a job! But when challenges or behavior problems come up and you don't know your WHY or have a solid sense of purpose, it's hard to keep going, much less spend time and energy trying to improve. And I think that's why so many teachers burn out in the first few years.

If I had a WHY at all during my first year of teaching, it was personal gain. I'm a very competitive person, and I set out to be the best teacher at the school. I wanted the best scores. I wanted to be the educator with all the recognition and awards. I was willing to work hard for it, and I often stayed at school till 9:00 p.m. My work ethic blinded me to reality. I thought that because I was working hard, my kids were learning and had everything they needed. I had built up my own confidence to the point it probably came off as arrogance. *I'm absolutely killing it. I'm very prepared, I have great lessons, and my classroom is rigorous. My kids are plowing through the content; they're going to be great readers.* Those were my thoughts.

For those first two years, I taught standards instead of students. I know now that's a dangerous mentality (and I speak out against it). Because I was looping with my students, I finally had an epiphany about the power of relationships during my third year with them. I asked myself, *Am I giving these kids what they need? Am I seeing the whole child or just the*

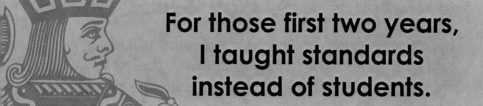

For those first two years, I taught standards instead of students.

academic student? My answers inspired me to re-assess what I was doing and chart a new course. Today, I check in with myself often enough to make sure my WHY is about my students and their futures. I'm especially motivated by research that shows literacy is the key to breaking a cycle of poverty. I want to be sure I'm giving my students the foundation they need to succeed in life.

My story is at the other end of the spectrum from Wade's because he always had a clear understanding of his WHY. He had lived it. He'd *been* that struggling kid who needed his teachers to see him as an individual and to support him. I had kids in my classroom who lived that reality as well, yet it took a while before I finally learned that I had to see all their realities, not just my own. This is why assessing where you are is so important. You have to know your purpose so you can adjust it when you get off track. Confidence is essential to a creative breakthrough, but sometimes an overabundance of confidence becomes a roadblock.

WADE: Teachers, coaches, and my friends were my only positive role models while I was growing up. They were the only people who remained a constant presence while my family was drifting in and out of the picture. I decided to become a teacher because I truly wanted to give back. I wanted to support other struggling kids who might not succeed—or survive—without good role models. That was my purpose, and I needed that strong sense of my WHY to work my way through college without much support. My WHY kept me going, even when I was ready to give up and spend my life working on a landscaping crew or in a barbecue restaurant.

I wasn't confident as a new teacher. I had a good work ethic (it had been modeled for me by the fathers of my closest friends) and that resulted in good test scores. But I was still trying to figure it all out, and I didn't feel like I was a fantastic teacher. I started out knowing my WHY. Even so, I lost track of that sense of purpose from time to time. For a while my WHY was about coaching because I wanted to be a friend and mentor to the kids. During my third year, I forgot my WHY because I was concentrating on test scores. I'd always had some of the best scores in South Carolina, and I started to

Hope, Wade, and one of their students, Amari, having a blast at Disney World

think, *Wow, it's a lot of pressure to keep that up.* I started teaching to the test and focusing on standards—when I should have kept my focus on relationships with my students.

You always have to ground yourself. You have to make sure your true purpose is at the center of everything you do in the classroom. You have fifteen to forty kids in your classroom, and they're human beings with their own struggles. When you step into the classroom, your WHY becomes their WHY, so you should be clear about what you're offering to them. Hope and I are completely aligned in this viewpoint. I think about that often, how we came from extremely different backgrounds and upbringings, but we both ended up at the same place.

Wade, Jaydon, and Alec taking in the rich history of the Roman Colosseum

On a fun outing with one of Hope's former first-grade students (he's an eighth-grader in this photograph) and his family. Hope's mother Pam couldn't miss out on the fun.

Your WHY may be different from ours, and it may have changed since the first day you stepped into your classroom. The truth is, there are a lot of reasons why people choose education as a career and then decide to remain there.

- Some people decide to teach because they have a strong interest in math or history or science and want to immerse themselves in their topic. The challenge then becomes igniting the same passion in their students.

- Some people love athletics and get an education degree because they want to coach. Sometimes these teachers come to life in the gym or on the practice field, but have less energy in the classroom—perhaps because they know more about engagement through sports than through creative instruction strategies.

47

- Some people want to be teachers because they love kids. Well, loving children is a big part of what teachers do, but it's a small part of the everyday reality. Affection doesn't replace content and academic rigor.

- Some people are attracted to what they see as flexibility in education: They want to have summers off or be on the same time schedule as their own children.

- Some people see teaching mainly as a paycheck and a retirement plan. Everyone has to do something for a living, so why not teach?

Do any of those scenarios reflect your own reason for becoming a teacher? Has your WHY changed since you made that initial career choice? Maybe it's time to re-evaluate your purpose.

Why You Need to Know Your Why

It seems like teachers feel worse about themselves these days than they ever have before. Resources and support are often lacking. For many teachers, the constant debate about educational reforms feels demoralizing, and the current evaluation systems have them second-guessing themselves. When teachers don't have a strong WHY in the face of all these new demands, their desire to be strong, effective educators starts to evaporate. We all *need* that power of purpose to keep us going strong. Without it, young teachers burn out and leave education within a few years. Others may spend twenty-five years in a classroom, doing the same thing over and over again without a sense of their WHY. You can easily recognize those teachers—they're the ones with the laminated lesson plans, more interested in preserving the status quo than in trying anything new.

Hope and Wade took some of their students to Hope's parents' house in South Carolina to experience the total eclipse and, of course, have a swim party!

There's a huge problem with not knowing your purpose. As a teacher, your WHY drives your students' educational WHY. Your job is to provide those kids with their own reason and purpose for sitting in a classroom from kindergarten through twelfth grade—again, other than the fact that they *have* to be there. If you don't know your own purpose as an educator, how can you pass along a sense of purpose to your students? If you're in the classroom showing kids how to memorize facts for the test, then that's what education will be to them—just a score at the end of the year. That's about teaching standards, not students. If your purpose is to equip students with intellectual curiosity and a love of learning, you'll find ways to go beyond the standards. (And we'll help you, so keep reading!)

Lately we've seen another WHY pop up along with the rise of social media. As we scroll through the "must follow" teacher accounts on Pinterest or Instagram, we end up feeling downright incompetent, looking at all the bright and shiny things posted there. Maybe you can relate to that awful feeling of not being good enough (or creative enough). We could probably duplicate some of those lessons, but they'd be all wrong for our students. Trying to measure up to Instagram is not a good WHY. Neither is a quest for recognition and another pat on the back. Recognition is nice, but it shouldn't be the only thing that fuels you, because you'll need to keep going even when you're not recognized for your efforts. Ultimately, your students should be central to your WHY. The power of your purpose must be strong enough to energize your teaching efforts, empower your class, and catapult each student toward academic success—and beyond.

Take some time now to reflect on your WHY—the one you started with in your career, the one you're working with now, and the one you'd like to work toward. When you accept where you are right now, warts and all, you open yourself up to creative growth.

*When your desires are strong enough,
you will appear to possess superhuman
powers to achieve.*

—Napoleon Hill

*Passion is one great force that unleashes
creativity, because if you're passionate
about something, then you're more
willing to take risks.*

—Yo-Yo Ma, Acclaimed Cellist

CHAPTER FIVE

Desire

♥ ♠ ♦ ♣

**Let desire drive your commitment
to challenge yourself and step
outside your comfort zone.**

W ho can listen to the soundtrack of *Hamilton* without getting choked up over the lyrics to "Dear Theodosia" every time it plays? This song is a heartbreaker. As the characters of Alexander Hamilton and Aaron Burr welcome their respective children into the world, they sing about laying a strong foundation for the generation that will come of age with a new nation. In their minds, the Revolution has become an opportunity to make the world a better place for these two infants.

Although they are political rivals—and, in the end, mortal enemies—Hamilton and Burr are united in their desire to give their children meaningful lives. They commit to whatever it takes to provide the right environment and opportunities for their kids so the children can leave their own marks on the world someday. These two men, both orphaned early in life, know all about the luck of the draw and the struggles that result from being dealt a weak hand in childhood. As a result, they are motivated to literally change the world for the sake of the next generation.

Wow.

There is so much we could say here. First of all, this is an exercise in engagement! *Hamilton* makes history hip, fun, and accessible. But our main point is that children deserve this move-the-world level of commitment from the adults in their lives—not just from their parents but from teachers as well. It's not enough just to show up and teach. You have to feel that strong sense of purpose and really let it consume you before you can create a learning experience your students will never forget.

That's why *desire* is the next step in your creative breakthrough. To develop that unwavering sense of purpose, that whatever-it-takes attitude, you start by *wanting* to be a more effective educator. Once you've self-assessed and accepted where you are, you may discover that desire pops up spontaneously. That's how we've often felt after reflecting on criticism. Once we acknowledge we have room for improvement (and who doesn't?), the lightbulbs start flashing all over the place. Suddenly we come up with a million ideas for things we want to try.

By now we hope you, too, have a desire to stretch, grow, and improve. But we need to warn you that change requires sacrifice. It helps to realize that up-front. Even small changes come with some amount of sacrifice. You'll give up free time to focus on improving your craft. You'll relinquish a measure of control when you try out something new in the classroom. You'll sacrifice your confidence (temporarily!) when you move forward with an activity that makes you feel awkward or nervous. You'll give up a sense of certainty as you formulate dozens of questions that begin with *What if...*

If you're feeling the urge to challenge yourself or make even one small change, that's a sign of growth. What can you do to act on that desire? Sometimes it's best to set small goals and take baby steps, because when small efforts go well, those experiences strengthen the desire to improve.

WADE: When I was new to teaching, I was constantly reflecting on what I could do to make my teaching or my discipline better. I set high expectations for my kids because I wanted them to be prepared for whatever life threw at them. At first I was using a coaching mentality in the classroom, establishing a competitive atmosphere and pushing the kids to succeed. But it didn't work for all the kids, and I realized that something had to change. I needed a new mindset and a new strategy, so I started looking at what the other teachers were doing. I saw them doing some cool things in their classrooms—but even so, it took a while before I tried anything new myself, because I was low on confidence. In the end I knew I had to challenge myself as a teacher because if I didn't, my students wouldn't reach their potential. The desire to have that breakthrough caused me to act on my WHY, and that's what eventually led me to using music creatively in the classroom.

The advantage in starting with small changes is you're more likely to make small mistakes or come up against small setbacks. But at some point, you're going to take a bigger step and a bigger risk. You might even pour a lot of heart and soul into something that flops. It's okay. Remind yourself the very fact you took that step counts as a success in this process. Let progress, not perfection, feed your desire to improve. Don't let one bad experience kill your desire for a creative breakthrough.

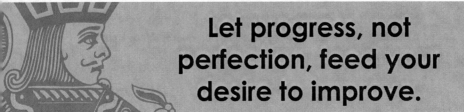

Let progress, not perfection, feed your desire to improve.

Don't Live in the Comfort Zone

We know people who willingly subject themselves to hours of strenuous exercise or whole weekends of back-breaking home renovation projects. They go through the physical discomfort because they're set on reaching a goal. But just try asking a guy who'd sign up for an Ironman without a second's hesitation to sing karaoke in front of a crowd or stand on a street corner wearing a clown costume. You're likely to be met with resistance. So many people avoid doing anything that feels unfamiliar, not because the task is particularly difficult, but because they can't handle internal discomfort. Believe us, we get it. We've been so far outside our comfort zones that we worried about being judged by a room full of twelve-year-olds. But, as writer Anne Lamott says, "It's good to do uncomfortable things. It's weight training for life." It's also a great way to get and hold your students' attention.

We hear the phrase "step outside the comfort zone" so often that it seems like a cliché. But the concept actually comes from the field of organizational psychology, where numerous studies quantify how the comfort zone affects job performance. There are three zones in the organizational psychology model, which we've adapted a bit and renamed for our own purposes. This is how we see the three-zone model as it relates to teachers:

- **The Comfort Zone**—If you spend a lot of time here, you probably don't have a problem with stress because you don't take many risks. You're in a familiar environment, you have a sense of control, and you encounter few surprises. You have a well-established curriculum, and you favor worksheets and "no-prep" activities for building academic skills. Lunchtime is for commiserating with your colleagues. Easy-peasy, right?

- **The Creative Zone**—This is where your breakthrough begins. It's where engagement begins. You feel right at home in your classroom because you've created a vibrant environment that suits you. You're usually happy to come to school. You sit with the students at lunchtime because you learn so much from them. Stress? Sure, but it's manageable. You get a little nervous when you have a new activity planned, but it helps you stay motivated.

- **The Panic Zone**—Let's face it, we've all been here at one time or another. The panic zone is characterized by rising anxiety, and if you spend too much time in this zone, you start thinking about leaving education entirely. You're overwhelmed by behavioral problems, morning tasks, papers to grade, content to review, new district rules, parent problems, and the list goes on—to the point you dread coming to work. The stressed-out emoji on your phone keyboard makes a frequent appearance in your text messages.

Organizational psychologists say it's normal to spend time in all three zones, with the best job performance and job satisfaction happening in the middle area that we call the creative zone. You don't have to be a certified creative genius to dwell here. It's all about a willingness to switch things up when you start feeling a little too comfortable.

WADE: My creativity in the classroom was tied to music and competitive games at first. Those things suited my personality as a musician, athlete, and competitor. I wasn't going to do anything corny like a room transformation because that was outside my creative boundaries. It was outside my comfort zone. Then one year we were getting ready for Parents' Day, and I had this idea to dress up in an Egyptian costume for my ancient civilization class. I'm not sure where it came from because I'd never dressed up for a lesson before. I mentioned it to Hope, and she was all over that idea. "If you're even thinking about it, then you need to do it," she said.

I loved the idea of surprising my kids. What could possibly throw them off more than having me show up in costume? But when the day came, I felt embarrassed. I think I might have been shaking, I was so nervous. As I was putting

on my costume, I was thinking, *What would my old coaching colleagues back home think of me right now?*

But it all worked out. There I was, teaching in that Egyptian costume, and the kids laughed, and they were engaged and attentive. The results were phenomenal, and the parents loved it too. They had no idea I'd never dressed up in character before, because I acted like I was completely at ease. (Fake it till you make it, right?) I wasn't just trying out a costume, I was trying out a whole new way of driving engagement. I got into education to make an impact on my students, so why not be unpredictable? The kids love anything that's a little bit crazy.

HOPE: We always try to attend out-of-school events that our kids or their parents invite us to. A few years back, we had an invitation to a birthday party, and as soon as we arrived I started sweating bullets. It was a huge dance party.

I took it all in, the deejay, the lighted dance floor, the music, all the kids (and even some adults) on the floor—and I just about broke out in hives because I don't dance. I knew the kids would try to get me on the dance floor, so I pulled out my camera and got real busy taking photos, hoping I could avoid that conversation.

Well, the kids weren't having it. They begged and begged me. They tugged at my clothes and pulled on my arm, trying to lead me out to the dance floor. "No, I'm fine; I'm just going to stand here and take lots of pictures because y'all just look so cute," I said. They were relentless! Even the parents told them, "Just leave Ms. King alone; she doesn't want to dance." After about twenty minutes, they gave up. *Whew!*

Then a single student approached me. Spencer was a sixth-grader whom I always pushed pretty hard. *Come on, Spencer, give me more. Be bold. Be confident. Step out of your comfort zone. Fake it if you have to, but give me more.*

"Can I talk to you, Ms. King?" he asked.

"Sure, buddy, what's up?"

"Ms. King, you're not doing any of those things you tell me to do every day. You tell me to be bold and step out of my comfort zone. But you're not doing that here."

Whoa! I had to take a step back because I'd just been schooled by a sixth-grader.

This was when I learned it's not about being perfect. It's not about having rhythm or all the right moves. It's about modeling what you preach. How can I ask my students to get outside their comfort zones if I won't do it myself? Now when our students are dancing, I dance with them. I pretend I don't feel self-conscious because I have no rhythm. And I do that every Friday afternoon because we always end our

> week with a little pep party. The kids love it. They're not judging my dance moves ... or perhaps sometimes they are! But who cares? I have fun. They have fun. And they appreciate my desire to build a relationship with them. If I have to step outside my comfort zone in the name of relationships, bring on the dance music.

We're asking you to join us in reconsidering your relationship with discomfort. Pick something that isn't characteristic of your teaching style—a costume, a song, or game—and then just rip off the proverbial bandage. Offer your students a learning experience that's different. Get comfortable with discomfort. You can expect to feel self-conscious or vulnerable when you put yourself out there, and that's okay. You may even find other teachers are giving you the side-eye because *they* are uncomfortable with anything different. No doubt some of your colleagues will be wondering why you suddenly need a song or a costume to teach your material. Well, the reason is engagement. Before long you'll have your students filled with anticipation, wondering what you're going to do next, eager to experience your next out-of-the-ordinary lesson. You'll be on your way to becoming the wild card.

First Step: A Smile

You can start your creative journey by changing just one thing. Even small changes can bring about outstanding results. So if you're still with us and still feel the desire, but you don't know where to start—and you're not ready to write a song—we're going to tell you about three starting points that are available to everyone.

These things are: a smile, passion, and enthusiasm. Sound too simple? Just stick with us.

These three things are natural starting points, because it's hard to make excuses about why you can't do them. They don't require time, money, props, or planning, so the barriers to implementation are minimal. It's not outwardly apparent that you're changing up something, so self-consciousness becomes less of an obstacle. You can work on any or all of these things no matter who you are, what your teaching background is, what kind of district you teach in, how small your budget is, or whether your administrator is supportive. Even so, the desire to change always comes with some amount of sacrifice, and these three things—a smile, passion, enthusiasm—are no exception. How big the sacrifice is will depend on where you're starting from. For some of us, any one of these things can be draining.

But let's start with that smile.

> **HOPE:** I think a lot of teachers feel like they're smiling when they're actually not. When you're a strong disciplinarian, that side can sometimes get the best of you. I got called on this once during an evaluation. An administrator whom I respected tremendously came into my room to observe a lesson. I was very confident. I just knew my content was strong and my classroom was a happy, vibrant place filled with enthusiastic students. I thought I absolutely killed it, and I expected nothing but positive feedback.
>
> Well, I got a surprise. When I met with my admin later, I got the expected praise on my content; that wasn't an issue. Then he said, "Hope, I have to be honest with you. Your expectations for your students are high, and that's okay. But here's the problem: You didn't smile, not once. Your students weren't smiling either."
>
> This comment devastated me more than I can tell you. I went home and cried for three days. That somber, unsmiling

educator is just not who I am, and it wasn't my intention to come off that way. In my mind, I had an environment filled with happiness and humor and joy—but in reality, I didn't have that at all. I told my mom about it. I talked to Wade about it. And once I pulled myself out of that dark pit of denial, I told myself, *I'm going to change this.* I used the sting of criticism to fuel my fire, and I began to work on my presentation. I taped my lessons and watched them later. I made a conscious effort to smile. I became very aware of and intentional about my demeanor and the environment I created. This one decision—simply to smile—launched one of the biggest professional growth spurts I've had, and my admin commented on the amount of positive change during my next evaluation. Plus, it's always nice to look out to your students and see them smiling as well. That's motivating. That's reason enough to continue.

Smiling is not just an expression of internal happiness. It's non-verbal communication, a way of setting the vibe in your classroom. A smile shows your interest in your students. It helps you to build positive relationships with them, because it makes you open and accessible. Since a smile is contagious, your students will smile too. There is a whole body of evidence, both in physiology and in psychology, that shows the act of smiling stimulates the reward centers in the brain at least as effectively as a chocolate bar, leading to a better mood overall—and minus the calories! That means a happy mood doesn't necessarily have to precede a smile; you can improve your mood and your outlook through the act of smiling.

If you're not naturally someone who smiles a lot, it can take a real effort to remember to smile every morning as your students enter the classroom. You might have "resting poker face" and not even know it, because you're happy inside and *feel* like you're smiling. Or you might be at a place in your life or in your career when you really don't feel like smiling. You may feel like you have no passion left for teaching, or that you have nothing to feel enthusiastic about. These can be very real personal barriers. But keep in mind that when you walk into your school every day, you sacrifice the mindset that it's all about you. Your mindset instead should reflect your purpose for being a teacher. It's about your WHY!

Every day, you sacrifice the mindset that it's all about you.

Researchers say it takes twenty-one days to set a new habit, so maybe the first change you make is a resolution to smile every day for three weeks, even when you don't feel like it. If you've ever tried to force a smile, you know it can be tough. It might even take some grit to get through twenty-one consecutive days. (That means you can't take weekends off!)

Rediscover Your Passion and Enthusiasm

When we talk about passion and enthusiasm in our workshops, teachers often ask about the difference between them. The two are closely related, but passion is internal, while enthusiasm is external.

Passion is intense interest or excitement for an activity or a cause. It's a motivating force. When you feel passion for something, you willingly invest your time and energy in it. Hobbies are an example of passion because you're putting your time and money into something that's not required to make a living. Do you sing in a choir? Volunteer at an animal shelter? Spend your weekends gardening? People sometimes become so motivated by and engaged in a hobby that it becomes part of their identity. They begin to define themselves as a marathon runner, or a poet, or a foodie. The activity isn't performed for a paycheck but for personal satisfaction. It's a way of indulging a passion.

When you were a new teacher right out of school, you probably had passion for your job. Remember the experience of fixing up your first classroom and the anticipation you felt as that first group of kids took their seats? Maybe you felt like you were embarking on your true calling, or that you had a chance to leave your mark on the world. If you're teaching specific content like science or history, you probably have—or at one time had—passion for that topic. But maybe you've started to lose touch with your sense of passion. It can be especially hard if you're an elementary school teacher who teaches every subject during the course of a school day. There's going to be at least one period of the day when you have to teach something you're not excited about. And that's where life as a teacher can get confusing. That's where you can lose sight of why you became an educator in the first place.

Be honest. How often have you thought to yourself, *I don't like the content I'm teaching today, so it's not going to be a good day.* Just like your WHY determines your students' WHY, your passion for your content affects your students as well. If you're not selling your content as fun and exciting, we can guarantee your students aren't buying it. Kids don't buy boring. They don't buy tedious. If you find yourself re-teaching the same content, or if your students aren't engaged, there's a good chance you're lacking either passion or enthusiasm.

So here's our crash course in Passion 101: You don't necessarily have to be passionate about fractions, or irregular verbs, or the chemical properties of all the elements, but you *do* have to be passionate about the way you present the material. This shift in mindset will drive you to liven things up with music or movement or games or whatever your forte is so your ordinary content becomes an extraordinary lesson. Remember those hobbies or interests that you're naturally passionate about? In Chapter Seven we're going to show you how to tap into them to amplify your content, like a laser that concentrates ambient light over and over again until it emerges in a single powerful beam. Your classroom will positively crackle with the energy. And— *BOOM!* That leads directly into enthusiasm.

When you have passion for your content and for educating kids, you show it with your actions—and that's enthusiasm. Enthusiasm is external. It's the way you reveal your internal passion to the people around you. It's the zeal and zest in your voice, the pep in your step, and the pizzazz in your lesson plans. It's the way you show your students the value in the content you're teaching. Your personal brand of enthusiasm is unique to you. The teachers at our school are all enthusiastic educators, yet they're all completely different from one another. Quiet, intense enthusiasm is just as powerful as animated, energetic enthusiasm.

Enthusiasm drives creativity. It shapes the environment and culture of your classroom. It's reflected in your room décor, the way you start each class, and the relationships you build with your students. When you teach with enthusiasm, you unleash an invisible, miniature hurricane in your classroom. Your enthusiasm fills the room, and your students get caught up in the vortex. They become excited about learning, the content whirls through their brains, and they remember the material, not because of their excitement about the content, but because of the way you taught it. Your enthusiasm is contagious.

WADE: Showing enthusiasm can be as simple as standing up and moving around the classroom. What do you do when your students are taking a test? There are plenty of times when I want to sit down and get a head start on grading papers. One day I thought, *No, I'm not going to do that. I'm going to walk around the room.* So that's what I did. And as I moved past the students, I rested my hand lightly on each of their shoulders for a second, just a light pat. I was doing it purposely and intentionally, and the kids really fed off that. It communicated to them that they're important to me and that I'm invested in their success. The energy in the room really ramped up, and I wasn't even doing anything crazy. I wasn't bopping around the room with my guitar or singing songs or anything like that. I was simply walking around the room while they were taking a test, but I was on my feet every minute until they were finished. Showing enthusiasm can start with small steps like that.

There are other benefits to teaching with enthusiasm. Enthusiastic teachers can build strong relationships with students because they see each child as a separate human being. They don't teach a classroom—they teach individuals. They are hopeful about each child's future and feel positive about each child's potential. They don't just say their students can change the world; they actually believe it.

They don't teach a classroom—they teach individuals.

When other educators come to visitation day at RCA, they invariably comment on how joyful our entire student body is. Many of them assume that, because we're a private school, our administrators cherry-pick kids with a certain attitude and demeanor. Yet nothing could be further from the truth. Our incoming fifth-graders are just regular kids from the public school system. They're just like your students, a mixture of children with various strengths and weaknesses and their fair share of problems and struggles. Here's our secret: It's not that we only admit joyful kids; it's that every adult in our building models passion and enthusiasm every single day. It truly is contagious.

Fake It till You Make It

Yes, it's a cliché. But we're going to say it anyway. Faking it is often necessary while you're getting the smile-passion-enthusiasm habit down. When you don't feel like it, just go into your classroom and smile. Even if you're not sure you've rediscovered your passion for education, act as if you have, or find a way to incorporate a personal passion into your curriculum. The same goes for enthusiasm—fake it if you have to. Just make a conscious and intentional effort to smile, tap into passion, project enthusiasm, and then just see what happens. Most likely the day will go better, and that will drive your desire to try it again.

Only you can determine what your own brand of passion and enthusiasm looks like. If this chapter is making you nervous because you're picturing enthusiastic instruction as being a teacher hopping around the classroom like a rabbit on acid, we can reassure you, that's not necessary! Your smile is as unique as your fingerprint. The same goes for the way you act on your internal passions and the way you exude enthusiasm. We're not asking you to fake anything that isn't authentic to you. Stick to your own brand of passion and enthusiasm, but rock it!

> **HOPE:** A lot of people think I'm really confident. They see all these crazy things I do in the classroom and assume that's just who I am and what I do. But the truth is, every time I get ready to do a room transformation, I question myself. Every time I change into a costume to teach a lesson, I question myself. I think it's just human nature to have some anxiety or doubt at the last minute. But if I get in front of my students and *act* like I feel awkward about my flapper costume—or the cheer or chant I'm introducing—then my kids will feel awkward about it too. That's when I have to fake my confidence. If I put out the vibe that I'm okay with what I'm doing, the kids just accept it too. They're excited because it's something different and unexpected, but they're ready to step into the roles I'm asking them to play because they see I'm at ease in my own role. We can never let our students know we feel awkward, even if we're freaking out inside, because those emotions are contagious.

Too often we hear teachers emphatically state they are not entertainers and that they did not become a teacher to entertain children. We see teaching differently. In our workshops, we ask teachers to entertain the notion that they are, indeed, entertainers—and if they can't accept that aspect of teaching, they may want to entertain the notion of a new profession. We want education to be the blockbuster act that's topping all the charts and breaking all the records! Now, clearly we're not talking about mindless entertainment. But when you step into your classroom, you take on a role, which, at the very least, should be your best version of yourself, no matter what kind of day you're having.

Think about a singer on tour, putting on an amazing concert night after night, belting out her greatest hits, joking with the band, raising cheers from a packed arena. Even as she sizzles on the stage, the tabloids report that her life is crumbling in any number of ways. She has to deliver that magical performance despite her personal heartaches because her audience bought into that event. Well, guess what? Your "audience" also holds a stake in your "event" every day, Monday through Friday. Just like that singer, you have to make magic for your students. You have to push aside outside factors and put on the best show you're capable of every time you walk into the classroom. It all begins with your face, your body language, your voice. Put on that smile, lose the monotone, and present your content with excitement and enthusiasm.

The smile-passion-enthusiasm trifecta is easiest to pull off on the days when the planets are aligned just right and you feel prepared to knock it out of the park. But what if you give it your best shot, the smile and passion and enthusiasm, but don't see immediate results? Then give it another go. You may be in a place where you feel broken, your family life is a disappointment, the dirty laundry is piled to the moon, and you forgot your lunch. Still, the fact is that you *have* to go to work; you have to be in that classroom every day from 8:00 to 4:00. Nothing is going to change that reality, so make the very best of it! You can't have a breakthrough without starting with one small change, so give that smile and passion and enthusiasm another try. And if you fake it long enough, guess what? Soon it won't feel like you're faking anymore; you will be *doing* it. Before long it becomes a habit. It's real, it's happening, and it's the first step toward positive change.

Educators are performers. *You* are a performer. You have your stage—how are you going to use it? Will you have a sold-out crowd? You should want that just as much as Britney Spears wants to play to a full house. (Is it just a coincidence that a "full house" is also a winning hand in cards?) When you begin a lesson, tell yourself, *It's showtime!* Pull in your audience so every single child is attentive and engaged, regardless of academic aptitude. Sell them all on the idea that learning is cool and knowledge is power. Sell the magic.

We are the stories we tell ourselves.

—Joan Didion

By three methods we may learn wisdom:
first, by reflection, which is noblest;
second, by imitation, which is easiest; and
third by experience, which is the bitterest.

—Confucius

CHAPTER SIX
Reflection

**Reflect on your own creative path.
What will it look like?**

So many teachers have asked us how we bring creativity into our classrooms that it's clear to us many educators would like to tap into that creative energy—if they only knew how. Believing in your own creativity may be a new mindset for you, and you may have doubts. That's to be expected. Before you make a big leap, take some time to reflect on the changes you'd like to make in your instructional style. You don't have to plan your entire journey all at once, but you'll need a general sense of your starting point before you can map out the first few steps.

Getting started on the creative path involves reflecting on the past: what kind of life you've had, your strengths, your experiences, your career path in education, and who you are outside the classroom. Take inventory of the skills you've acquired, hobbies you've pursued, goals you've reached, trips you've taken, and topics that interest you. All of these things form an inner well of inspiration that you'll draw from. That's why self-reflection is an essential ingredient in shaping your own personal brand of creativity.

Remember, on this path it's not so much the educational content we're focused on, but the delivery method. Since creative delivery drives engagement, you'll need to identify and develop the creative delivery style that works best for you. You'll be building on what you've already established as a teacher, but you should also be ready for change. (If you've been working from laminated lesson plans, you can toss those out now.) Can you borrow ideas from others? Absolutely. Just stay true to who you are.

If you're naturally a reflective person, this step will be easy for you. If you don't normally practice self-reflection, please don't skip past this step just because it's a mental exercise rather than something you can try in the classroom. Jot down notes on paper, if it helps you reflect on your life and your outside interests, or talk to someone who knows you well. This step is necessary and important; it relates back to student engagement as the purpose for your creative breakthrough.

Consider New Definitions of Creativity

If you don't see yourself as a creative person, you may want to reflect on how you define "creativity" so you can expand your view of it. Remember what we said in Chapter Three: When the Joker tries to convince you that you don't have a creative bone in your body, you don't have to listen to him.

In her book *Big Magic: Creative Living Beyond Fear,* author Elizabeth Gilbert talks about how intimidating the word "creative" can be and suggests replacing it with the word "curious." It's a good exercise, because we're betting that very few—if any—educators would claim they don't have a curious bone in their bodies. Hope often says her personal brand of creativity is all about hands-on learning because she is naturally nosy. When she's curious about something, she wants to pick it up, touch it, smell it, and examine it. Her nosiness and spirit of exploration are why the hands-on approach is often her go-to delivery method for the content she teaches.

People tend to define creativity in terms of making things, but creativity is often about *doing things.*

People tend to define creativity in terms of making things, but creativity is often about doing things.

We've briefly touched on the notion of lunchtime as a creative opportunity, so let's expand on that. You should jump on any opportunity to build relationships and get a little bit nosy about your students' lives and interests—both are key elements in your creative breakthrough. If you're taking baby steps, look for one thing to do differently. This is a great step to take. Too many teachers spend their lunch period or recess with other teachers making small talk, gossiping, and—let's be honest—complaining about how their day is going. Pull yourself out of that unproductive routine! Sit with a different group of students every day. Or eat your lunch quickly and then walk around, pulling up a chair to different tables for a few minutes. If you're teaching the younger kids, go out to the playground with them and swing or climb on the monkey bars. Consider the message it sends and what it does for children when their teacher comes out and sits on the swing beside them or takes a turn in the kickball game. The impact it can have is huge, and yet it's a rare event. *This* is the perfect way to create the unexpected and ensure all eyes are on you.

Building relationships with your students can translate into academic success because children want to try harder for you when they can see you care about them. (Think about the last time you went out of your way to do something for a boss who barely acknowledged your existence.) When you have a few minutes during lunch or recess, ask questions and really *listen* to your students. When you learn their favorite TV show is *Agents of SHIELD* or that they're in a race to catch the most Pokémon, file that information in your brain so you can dream up ways to bring superheroes and mythical pocket monsters into a lesson. In fact, if you just make a fleeting reference to something your kids are interested in, they're likely to sit up straight and listen harder because they're thinking, *OMG, she said Pokémon!* You'll have their full attention because you surprised them with your unexpected knowledge of the stuff they think is cool. And just like that, you've done it! You let your curiosity drive one small creative endeavor, which led to a moment of engagement, all because you've taken advantage of a creative opportunity.

Reflect on Your Vision for Change

The easiest way to guide your self-reflection about the changes you want to make is to see yourself in action. Set up a camera in the back of your room and record a few lessons. As you play them back, ask yourself, *Would I like to be in this class day in and day out?* If you have children or grandchildren, ask yourself if this is what you'd like their educational experiences to look like. If not, then it's time for a change—and it's never too late to make a change.

Now play the video again with the sound turned off. Without audio, you're not listening for the content, but rather watching the delivery. How many times did you smile? Does your passion or enthusiasm come across in your body language? What kind of energy do you project? If you were a student, would you buy what this teacher is selling?

What kind of changes are you ready to make? What would you like a taped lesson to look like a year from now or two years down the road? As you contemplate your vision for change, spend some time reflecting on the factors that will influence your path. These include the following elements.

Your Personality

Are you the kind of person who dips a toe into cold water, or do you dive right in? We're not going to discourage you from starting out ambitiously if that's who you are, but understand that baby steps are okay—it's perfectly fine to do one thing differently and see how it goes. Reflect on the pace that's right for you and will allow you to grow and stretch without tremendous amounts of stress. Consider how you bounce back from mistakes and disappointments. Do you think of yourself as a competitive person? If so, realize that you're only in competition with yourself and not with other teachers. You're measuring your progress and growth against your past efforts, going for your personal best. Reflect on any habits that tend to turn into self-sabotage (like perfectionism or procrastination) and realize the goal is progress and not perfection. If you procrastinate, does it reflect a deeply buried fear of failure or of looking foolish? How will you get past this?

The Grade and Subjects You Teach

Some teachers want to make these two things into obstacles. They say things like, "Math is not a creative subject," or "My high-school students are too old to play games in class," or "I have the same group of elementary students all day long, so it's impossible to surprise them." The truth is that those are excuses. (We'll show you examples of what creativity can look like in Chapters Seven and Eight.) Reflect on how you're approaching your grade level and content in terms of increasing engagement. We're the first to admit that younger kids are often the easiest to engage, while teens are more of a challenge. Still, we want you to realize that even if you can't wow middle-schoolers with wonder, you can surprise them with the unexpected.

Even if you can't wow middle-schoolers with wonder, you can surprise them with the unexpected.

Your Classroom Culture

Reflect on the relationships you have with your students and the relationships they have with their classmates. Are your students accountable to each other as well as to you? Do you all function well as a team, or can you put more effort into building and cultivating relationships? Think about your classroom culture in terms of respect, manners, tolerance, acceptance of differences, and the way students interact with one another. Do you create opportunities for them to learn about one another and collaborate in positive ways? Do you model what positive interaction looks like? Your creative efforts will go more smoothly if you've established a positive classroom culture.

Discipline

Reflect on your classroom management strategies. Do you have good control of your kids, or will you have to work on that before you can give them enough autonomy to do a hands-on learning project? It's a given that you can't introduce creative instruction methods without the proper level of classroom management. We're both very strict teachers, and we work hard to create a culture of discipline and respect in our classes. Where does discipline fit into *your* classroom culture? How does it align with the type of relationships you've built with your students?

Class Size

Be honest: are you making excuses about what you can or can't do because you have a large class? It may be a challenge, but ultimately it's your reality. If you're using class size as an excuse, can you change your mindset to view it as a roadblock that you must find a way around? Look at the ways other teachers deal with large classes and see what's successful (and what isn't) for them. We've both taught up to forty kids in one class, and our philosophy is that class size doesn't matter. We believe it's all about the quality and rigor of the instruction. Are you willing to accept that philosophy as well?

Student Demographics and Interests

We've already explained why the socioeconomic status of your students can never be an excuse for low engagement, whether you're dealing with Title I or helicopter parents. Now we want you to reflect on how your students' demographics and interests will shape your engagement efforts and how you will build relationships based on who they are and what they are interested in. Realize that even if your students and their families are very different from you, you can learn from one another and build relationships based on those differences.

Your Mindset

In Part One, we talked about the differences between a growth mindset and a fixed mindset. Reflect on where you are right now. Do you believe in your ability to flex your creative muscle and develop skill and confidence in this area? It helps to understand up-front that your personal brand of creativity is a work in progress; growth will come in spurts and may not always be linear. As Confucius said, "It does not matter how slowly you go as long as you don't stop." Realize that making mistakes and pushing through roadblocks is part of your path. You can model the growth mindset for your students by letting them see you take on challenges and try new things, even if you sometimes fall flat. This is also a good time to reflect on the "no excuses" mindset we talked about in Chapter Two. How will you get past obstacles without letting them trigger you back into a fixed mindset?

Reflect on Your Goals

For us, the creative path has been all about delivering content in a way that drives student engagement and stimulates a lifelong love of learning in our kids. We hope that reflects a large part of your personal goals as well. But you may have additional goals, so take some time to reflect on those. Are you feeling stuck in a rut? Looking for greater career satisfaction? Trying to step up your game after receiving a lukewarm evaluation? (If so, good for you! You've assessed your current situation and decided to act.) Thinking about your priorities can help you determine your path, your pace, and your purpose.

Does your goal include continual growth? It's good to understand up-front that if you develop a creative lesson that works now, it may not work forever. Or if you do the same thing over and over again, you may lose your enthusiasm for it no matter how creative and exciting it was the first time. (We'll show you how to build on your efforts and level up existing activities in Chapter Eight.) Are you willing to renew your commitment to growth every time you find yourself feeling very comfortable?

When you reflect on your goals, remember this: *Ultimately, results are what matter.* Whatever methods you use, the reality is that you have to get to a point where you can prove they are working. There is a good reason administrators regard games or room transformations as fluff. It becomes fluff when the environment is not paired with *rigorous content.* As you think about the ways you're going to make your classroom activities engaging and exciting, you must also consider how you're going to incorporate challenging standards and content-driven focus. There is simply no other option. In the end, the costumes and the props and the songs are just enhancements. The heart of the lesson is always going to be standards and academics. We'll go over the Rules of Rigor in Chapter Seven. You'll be amazed at how simple they are.

This self-reflection step is also the point at which you should examine your attitudes about standardized testing. Teachers complain about testing all the time and say they spend too much time preparing students for tests. If you currently see standardized testing as an obstacle to the way you want to teach, we feel you. But the reality is that, in every profession, people have to demonstrate their effectiveness. In our profession, results are measured through standardized testing. It's unlikely that standardized testing is going away any time soon, so we hope you can find a way to come to terms with this reality rather than complain about it. Remember, content (standards) is what you're selling, but it's the delivery (your creative approach) that determines whether or not your students are buying. Try to think of those test scores as your sales goal. (More on this in Chapter Nine!)

Okay, we've thrown a lot at you here, and it was probably a little heavy. We're glad you stuck with us, and we hope you'll go back over this chapter at some point and really put some thought into the things we covered. But for now, we're moving on to our favorite topic: engagement. The fun starts here!

Provide an uncommon experience for your students and they will reward you with an uncommon effort and attitude.

—Dave Burgess, *Teach Like a Pirate*

Good teaching is one-fourth preparation and three-fourths theater.

—Gail Godwin, novelist

CHAPTER SEVEN

Engagement

Develop a new understanding of engagement.

It breaks our hearts to hear students of any age claim they hate school. How does that happen? For starters, one survey of high-schoolers who dropped out found that 47 percent said school was boring. Two out of three said their classes did not motivate or excite them. For these kids, the problem wasn't the academics—it was the monotony that pushed them out the door without a diploma. And this is exactly why we see engagement in terms of that sell-out concert you can't bear to miss, the twirling ballerina you can't take your eyes off of, or the monkey juggling bananas on a bicycle. Engagement is big and bold and captivating—but most importantly, it is memorable.

Think of a special time in your life. It might be your first trip to Europe, a spectacular meteor shower, or the moment your child was born. How many details come to mind? Can you conjure up the sights, sounds, smells, and feelings all over again? We're betting you can. Everyone has those memories that stick like glue. And that's how education should be for our kids: a series of learning experiences they can never forget because we, as educators, created a greatest-hits reel of magical moments for them.

Too many teachers are using worksheets to teach difficult concepts. They see their students at work, all those heads bent over all those desks, and mistakenly believe this equals engagement. If you're shooting for that sold-out crowd, worksheets will never be the answer. They will never make students *want* to be at school. Don't believe us? Think back to the last time you filled out an income tax form. Were you sad when it was done? Did you wish you could fill out a tax form every day? Of course not! It's more likely you were desperately wishing for the process to be over so you could get that big fat tax refund check for all your classroom-related deductions (tongue planted firmly in cheek). The bottom line is that worksheets do not create memorable learning experiences or lifelong learners; instead, they lead to tuned-out kids who'd rather be doing anything else. We know about the long-term effects of this firsthand because we live it every day in our marriage.

> **HOPE:** This is often a source of embarrassment to me, but I barely know anything about the world or our nation's history. In college history classes, I was always bored. I never had instructors who made the subject come alive, so I didn't care about it—and as a result, I didn't learn a dang thing. I'd skip class whenever I could. I'd memorize facts and cram for the test so I could keep my scholarship, but after the test, every bit of knowledge would vanish from my brain—*POOF! GONE!* Wade is always shaking his head because I know so little about politics. He makes me sit down and watch the news every night because that's his thing, and he wants to share it with me. And now I teach at a global school where we promote current events and cultural studies as an important part of our curriculum, and I'm out of my league. Kids approach me wanting to talk about events that have piqued their curiosity and I have to duck the conversation—I may as well be making a lame excuse about having to wash my hair! This is part of the reason I'm so passionate about engagement now.

Both of us try to avoid using worksheets in the classroom because students are not stimulated by them. Plain and simple, worksheets are not engaging. (To be clear, it's not the content on the worksheets that's the problem, but rather the monotonous delivery. Hope uses an adaptation of the Hungry Hippos tabletop game in her classroom that is basically a worksheet on steroids. Changing up the delivery method makes the content engaging.) When you pour all your efforts into worksheets, standards, and assessments, your students want to run away from your classroom instead of into it. When kids are bored, they may be "working," but they're not retaining anything. What will become of the world if we have a whole generation of young adults who tuned out, and now, as a result, don't understand the political process or the mistakes of history? Has that question ever been scarier than it is today? Let's rally the troops! Let's *all* focus our time and energy on engagement! Why not create magical classrooms everywhere—where students run in the door every single day, filled with anticipation?

Okay, now that we've got you all pumped up, we're going to rein you back a bit with a reality check: *To meet your scholastic goals, engagement must be paired with academic rigor.*

The Rules of Rigor

There are two basic Rules of Rigor, and they're very simple to remember and apply when you're planning an activity:

Rule #1: Go for application instead of memorization.

Rigor is not how fast you cover your material or how much your kids can memorize for the test. Memorization results in word vomit— students spewing out definitions and facts on command without being able to make real-world connections. Then they come back from summer break, and it's like they've regressed two grade levels because they've forgotten it all. It's far better to focus less on memorization or cramming for a test and more on application by allowing students to use skills and concepts through hands-on, higher-level-thinking activities.

Here's an example: Hope uses a homemade version of the Hedbanz party game to teach ELA skills. If you're not familiar with it, it's a quiz game in which one player uses a stretchy headband to hold an answer card on his forehead where he can't see it, while the other players feed him clues until he guesses what's on the card. When Hope started out, her version of the game required the kids to define terminology like "simile" and "metaphor." Then she recognized that she was only getting word vomit out of the kids—memorized definitions. Now, when the students play Hedbanz, they have to quickly think up an example of a simile or metaphor to score a point. In other words, they have to apply their knowledge of the terminology. Instead of regurgitating *a figure of speech involving a comparison between two things using "like" or "as,"* they're required to make up a sentence containing a simile, like *He's quick as a fox.* The application of knowledge changed the rigor of the lesson completely.

We're also busting the myth that fun and excitement alone equals engagement. Yes, we like to stress that teachers can build engagement by doing something different and becoming masters of the unexpected. Well, if you threw a pizza party with a deejay and a disco ball during math class, that would be different and memorable—and no doubt your kids would be excited. But it's not engagement if they're not learning something. The engagement factor must enhance your content, not detract from it. Engagement goes beyond creating a fun environment. If you are going to work at thinking outside the box and stepping outside your comfort zone, you want to get the biggest bang for your buck. The Rules of Rigor are the key.

Rule #2: No student becomes invisible; everyone is accountable.

Let's break down this rule with an example: We once told a group of students we were going to play Jeopardy to review for a test. They were squealing with excitement as we split them up into teams and brought up the first question on the screen. Within just a few rounds we sensed we had a problem. Can you guess what it was? Yep, the smartest kid on each team answered every question. The other kids didn't even try—*because they were focused on winning the game.* They weren't in it to learn; they were happy to score points by relying on the kid who already knew all the answers. So what did the students learn that day? *Nada*. Zip. Zilch. The advanced learner who had already mastered the content didn't learn anything new. And the kids who piggybacked on his knowledge sure didn't master the content either, because they had become "invisible" in the game. It was a waste of instructional time and an epic teacher fail. But hey, the students sure had a good time!

We both often use games in our classrooms. But we now have the second rule of rigor to make sure the students are learning while they're having fun. We can break down this rule even further. When we say "No student becomes invisible," this is what we mean: *There is no waiting for a turn, and no way to strike out.*

Gone are the days when students answer one question and then wait six rotations until their next question comes up. Gone are the days when a wrong answer puts a student out of the game and on the sidelines as a bystander. We can't have kids answering just four questions in forty minutes or being eliminated during the first round. Now when we play Jeopardy, all the students answer independently on their own whiteboards. Every single student is accountable for every single question and answer. Then we check answers as a group and if *everyone* is correct, the team earns a point.

We encourage you to use games in your classroom, but please make sure that *all* students are engaged at all times. Even the kids who no longer have a chance of winning should be getting academic content—and value—from the game. You don't want kids striking out and then just sitting there for twenty or thirty minutes doing nothing. We can guarantee you there will always be those kids who figure out how to strike out on purpose, just so they won't have to participate.

The Rules of Rigor allow you to work smarter rather than harder because you can more effectively teach challenging content with an engaging activity. It's all about doing the most possible with the time you have. On the other hand, when you teach content that your students are naturally interested in and engaged with, there's no need to make extra work for yourself by designing special activities. You can safely rely on your regular teaching for those units; just be sure to infuse your instruction with a smile, passion, and enthusiasm. Keep in mind that the extra effort you put into special activities for the less interesting content (or content that is difficult to grasp) will pay off *when you only have to teach it once!* This is the power of creating a memorable experience for your students—they will remember those algebraic equations, or the rules for punctuating different types of clauses, when you teach in ways that hold their attention.

Are you still with us? Okay then, moving on! We've broken down engagement into four essential ingredients to make the concept easier to digest:

- Expectations
- Environment
- Energy
- Empowerment

Please notice that "expense" is not included with those four *E*s! As we told you in Chapter Two, your budget is not a valid excuse for why your students are bored. You don't have to spend a lot of money to create engagement. There are many things you can do with inexpensive props or borrowed items—trust us! We're going to show you how while we take a closer look at the four *E*s.

Set Your *Expectations* High and Don't Accept Less

Before you start experimenting with creative instructional strategies, you absolutely must lay a strong foundation by setting your expectations for your students' behavior. Anything less and you risk total chaos. It will ruin your day, and you don't need one more opening for the Joker to mess with your mind. Have your classroom management practices in place, and establish a certain level of trust in your students so they don't lose control when the excitement level rises. It's not enough to set rules; you also must enforce them consistently.

For us, one of the most important classroom rules is respect for the speaker. No matter who is speaking, whether the teacher or another student, everyone else in the room must focus on that person. We don't want eyes wandering to the ceiling, the window, or the clock on the wall. And we most certainly don't want side conversations or disruptive fidgeting. Whenever we sense a shift of attention or an air of restlessness in our classes, we refocus everyone with a call and response. It can be as simple as calling out, "Jamie has the floor!" and your students responding with, "Ooh, track her!" as they shift their attention back to the speaker—but you can get as creative or as silly as you'd like. Wade calls out, "Sharkbait!" and his students respond with "Ooh-ha-hah!" as they shake their hands in the air and then immediately snap back to attention (inspired, of course, by the movie *Finding Nemo*). Please don't fall into that old trap of saying, "I'll wait … " and then wasting precious minutes counting out loud as your class settles down at its own pace. Your kids will think, *Good! How long?* and you'll slowly turn into a skeleton while they test your limits.

There is a secret to making this call-and-response technique work, and it's the same secret for just about everything else we do. Any teacher can create magic in any classroom, because the key to magical learning experiences is tied to just one thing. It's not tied to budget, class size, or any other factor; rather, it depends on that one factor that every single one of us can control. It's the most valuable card in your deck, the one that can change your hand into a full house! Can you guess what it is?

Consistency.

The key is consistency. The expectation you set on the first day of class—and we urge you to set the bar high—is the expectation you'll have to maintain every day for the rest of the school year. So each time you call out, "Sharkbait!" you have to stick to the expectation of an energetic response and an immediate snap to attention. Anything less than that and you do it again—and again, if necessary—until you get the response you established up-front.

Of course, the reality is much harder than the simple concept. If consistency were easy, we'd all be rocking it. It's easy to maintain consistency and expectations on a great day. When you've just taught a killer lesson and can practically see the synapses firing in your students' brains, when you're on top of the world, when you have dinner in the crockpot, when the unexpected has happened and all your laundry is folded (if you're like us, maybe it's not put away … but let's celebrate the fact that it's folded), it's easy to hold your class accountable. On days like that, if you do a call and don't get a response with the level of enthusiasm you're looking for, you just say, "Nope, we're doing that again. Sharkbait!" On those days, you're ready to call it ten times if necessary to get your class to meet your expectation.

But then there are those other days. You know the ones we mean. Those days when your alarm clock doesn't go off, you're having a bad hair day, your principal is on your back, you definitely don't have dinner ready—and, as a matter of fact, your family hasn't had a home-cooked meal all week. The teacher problems are piling up, and on those days when you call, "Sharkbait!" and get a response that ranks about four on an enthusiasm scale of one to ten, you take the easy way out. You're simply too tired to say it one more time. You figure level four is good enough for today, so you let it go and move on. Well, guess what you've just done? You've taken the bar of expectation and lowered it from a ten to a four. Congratulations—four is the new expectation you've set and your new level of high. You aren't ever getting back to your initial ten. *If you want to create magic, you must NEVER settle for "good enough," because that's what your students will become.*

If you want to create magic, you must NEVER settle for "good enough," because that's what your students will become.

Whatever expectation or rule you implement, whether it's respecting the speaker, the way students answer questions, or how they respond to criticism, it's never going to work without consistency. You have to maintain clear and consistent expectations on the days you're rocking your teacher role as well as on the days you're struggling. Even on those bad days, push for that level of excellence. You might be gritting your teeth. You might feel sweat running down your back. It might take every ounce of your strength to fake it—and you're not sure you're ever going to make it. Remember that just because you don't feel it in your heart or mind doesn't mean that you're exempt from showing enthusiasm on the outside.

If you can't push through the bad days and enforce your rules with consistency, it will be hard to create magic in your classroom. Without consistency, you essentially become two different teachers. You're like Dr. Jekyll and Mr. Hyde to your students—they don't know which version of you will walk through the door each day. So the next time you're impatient with your class or frustrated because you can't get your students to a certain level, ask yourself if it's because you've given them two very different sets of expectations. If you have to admit to yourself that inconsistency is the root of the problem, devise a plan to keep yourself on track—even when you hit one of those rough days.

Anytime you implement something new, plan on it taking a while to stick. Remember, it takes all of us (teachers and students) about twenty-one days to form a new habit. This is where you need the grit to stick it out. Do not show your students that you'll give up and move on if they don't get it right in the first week! And don't listen to the Joker when he whispers, *That will never work.* Push through the challenge. Cue the sweat ... cue the blood ... cue the tears ... and stand firm with your expectations until they're set in stone. Laying the groundwork isn't always easy, but it's worth it. Consistency is the first ingredient in the secret formula for making magic.

Create an *Environment* That Furthers Your Goals

Your classroom environment is a huge part of student engagement. But environment pertains to more than just the actual physical space and the classroom décor. You also create a specific type of learning environment through classroom management strategies, relationships, and classroom culture. Engagement happens when you establish an environment that is relevant to your students, reflects their interests and yours, promotes learning, and is both visually and emotionally appealing.

We believe strongly in the power of environment, not only for students but for *you.* We'd like to see more teachers incorporating their passions and interests into their classroom décor instead of just tacking up generic posters and charts. If you're anything like us, you probably have days when you spend as many waking hours in your classroom as you do in your home. You should feel energized and excited when you walk into your classroom every day, ready to teach in a manner you feel passionate about. Otherwise it's just another job. So yes, your students should love the vibe in your classroom, but you probably need to love it even more and to truly feel at home there.

A lot of teachers recall the excitement of walking into their first classroom—so many possibilities! They poured their hearts and souls into decorating it in anticipation of all those young learners streaming through the door on the first day of school. But sometimes the décor never evolves past that point. When we started teaching in South Carolina, we saw all too many faded posters that looked as if they'd been hanging in the same place for thirty years. An environment like that is stagnant; it can't possibly contribute to engagement. So take a peek behind some of the items hanging on your classroom walls. If the paint is a different color back there, it's probably time for a change. Classroom décor should grow dynamically along with you and your students.

> **HOPE:** I came up with an oldies musical theme for my first classroom in Pendleton Elementary. I had a life-size cardboard cutout of Elvis, and I used my dad's old 45s in different ways for the décor. I loved the nostalgia and the personal connection, even if my first-graders didn't really relate to it. To bring their interests into the room, I had a "celebrity wall" with pictures I'd cut from magazines of their favorite pop stars. There was a frame in the center of the wall where I'd place a photo of a different student each week—and we would celebrate that student and learn more about him or her. Everyone was included; everyone had a turn. I didn't make it an academic or behavioral reward because we all know there would be more than a few kids who'd never make

it to the celebrity wall. Instead, it was about building relationships and a classroom family.

At some point, it dawned on me just how many of my students were latchkey kids—they were taking care of siblings
even younger than they were! That's when I adopted a pair
of guinea pigs. Having animals in the classroom is a form of
experiential learning, but our classroom pets went beyond
that. They were a way to support my latchkey kids with life
lessons about caring and responsibility.

Today, my classroom décor is based on my love of reading. It has a book motif, fairy tale elements, and an *Alice in
Wonderland* theme. I did it on a budget, which meant comb-
ing through thrift stores and talking my grandparents out

of a beautifully bound set of old encyclopedias. I infused my crafty side by making a lot of the Wonderland elements myself. Wade says it looks like Hobby Lobby threw up on my walls—and I have to admit, it's true! Mainly I want my classroom to bring reading to life for my students. I want to show them that opening a book is like stepping into another world. Books can take us on adventures we'll never have in our own lifetime—like falling through a rabbit hole to Wonderland.

WADE: I was really uncertain how to decorate my first classroom at Townville Elementary. I'm a typical guy; I didn't know where to begin, so Hope and her mom stepped in. The school had an overall theme of "Under the Sea," so the ladies brought in fishing nets, treasure chests, and plenty of stuffed sharks—or maybe they were dolphins. And I didn't say anything because I wasn't about to hurt anyone's feelings, but I never felt at home teaching in that room. At the time, I was head wrestling coach for the district, and my guys would come in and say, "Mr. King, you're the coach. Why do you have stuffed animals everywhere?" By the time I moved over to Pendleton, I'd learned my lesson: When you shove yourself into a mold that doesn't fit, you'll never be happy. This time, I fixed up my classroom by myself. I love superheroes, so I had a comic book theme and made shadowboxes containing superhero costumes for the walls. It changed everything about the way I felt in my environment.

My classroom today has a *School of Rock* theme. It has a low stage and big speakers, and I love walking around with a guitar and singing songs with my kids. There's a drum set in

the middle of my classroom, and each year a designated student sits there instead of at a regular desk, taking notes and participating in class. That student is also in charge of drumming. He knows when he's supposed to drum, like during a cheer or chant, or when I ask for a low drumroll to build energy. We also take brain breaks where I'll play for a minute and the students get up and do a few dance steps and then we all get back to work. The role of "classroom drummer" has become a huge part of my learning environment.

Do you see a classroom makeover in *your* future? Maybe it will be part of your creative breakthrough. If so, start small (or go big if you want) but definitely introduce some personal elements. Decorating your classroom in a way that pleases you is not selfish. It helps you build relationships with your students by sharing a bit of yourself with them. And when your environment feeds your passion and sets your soul on fire, how could that flame not carry over to your students? Enthusiasm spreads like wildfire.

Yet another way to foster engagement through the classroom environment is what we call a classroom transformation. This is where we bring in props, backdrops, sound effects, and whatever else we need to magically transport the students to a whole different environment—like a sandy beach, a spy lab, or an animal safari. It takes excellent classroom management to make this instructional strategy work. But when your students walk into *Jurassic World* or a *Super Mario* video game, you are guaranteed immediate engagement. Transforming a classroom takes a bit of effort and planning, so we save them for the most difficult or most boring topics when we need

Kim Bearden and Hope soaking up the fun in their beach room transformation

help with engagement the most. Hope is well known for her creative room transformations; she blogs about them and shares photos and tips on social media. But, interestingly enough, we both got started doing room transformations for different reasons.

HOPE: While I was teaching at Pendleton, I found my students lacked the background knowledge to understand certain concepts—all because they'd never been outside their hometown, much less the state of South Carolina. One day I gave them a writing prompt: *If you could go anywhere in the world, where would it be, and why?* And—quite the eye-opener—more than 80 percent of the kids answered either Dollar General or Walmarts (with an *s*—we're in the South, y'all!). They literally had no sense of the outside world. It just about broke my heart. And it speaks to the importance of getting to know your students. How can you reach them if you don't know where they are in the game of life? In this case, I figured if I couldn't take them out to the real world, I could bring the real world to them.

An opportunity came when our class did a unit on rocks and minerals, and I discovered many of my kids had never walked in the sand—despite the fact our school was less than three hundred miles from Myrtle Beach. After a few days of blank stares, I knew that pictures would never do what an experience could. I couldn't build my students' knowledge and expect them to retain it if there was nothing for that knowledge to stick to. So I decided to do a room transformation that a colleague, Kim Bearden, had posted about online. (Oh yes, we borrow and steal ideas too!) I transformed my room into an oceanside beach, where the kids could let sand run through their fingers and hear the crashing waves and the call of the gulls overhead (a soundtrack from a relaxation CD). I was trying to tap into all five senses, so I even had them put sunscreen on for the scent. Even though my students couldn't actually wade in the surf, I wanted to give them an ocean experience that would allow them to make connections with new content and facts.

WADE: Although I am married to the guru of room transformations, I really had not planned on ever doing one on my own. I don't have the crafting skills to decorate a room like Hope does. I can envision something that would look cool, but I don't know how to pull it off. Then I hit a point where I was really feeling the monotony of repetition. The excitement just wasn't there anymore. I had helped Hope set up her props and backdrops several times when she transformed her classroom, so I asked her if we could collaborate on a room transformation that would include content from both our areas. I wanted to stretch myself a bit, see what else I could do for the engagement factor, and maybe step outside my comfort zone. At the same time, I wanted to go into it with someone who knows what she's doing. We decided to pool our efforts on a mixed-content lesson with a *Jurassic World* theme—and it was awesome! Hope covered the walls, transformed tables that seat four students into "jeeps," and created really cool props, like a dinosaur's nest. We played the movie theme along with sound effects of growls and roars. The kids were so excited that they didn't even want to take restroom breaks—yet the content was really tough. Standards? We were hitting them out of the park. We must have pulled in ten different standards. It was a great day for everyone, especially for me! I'd helped Hope with the grunt work on her transformations so many times (have to keep my wife happy!), and I finally got to find out what it's like to teach in a transformed environment. I'm not going to lie; I loved it! And the fact that I got to dress like Chris Pratt, the hero of the movie, was definitely a bonus.

When Hope does a really elaborate room transformation, she'll often leave it up for a week or three and pair the décor to a big-themed unit or teach across content areas. Our *Jurassic World* transformation pulled in science content about animal classifications, adaptations, life cycles, food webs, and food chains. In order to "escape" from *Jurassic World*, our sixth-graders had to complete a series of math and ELA challenges. The two of us dressed in adventure gear, and we helped our students step into their role as researchers by giving them headlamps. (Hope made them by hot-gluing inexpensive push lights from the dollar store to stretchy headbands.) The kids were completely engaged, even with the math problems. We introduced math periodically throughout the four-hour lesson by blaring a siren and telling the kids, "There's a crisis situation here in Jurassic World! You can only avert disaster by solving the problem on the board!" They would immediately pause their scientific classification tasks and give their full attention to the math puzzle—because who wants to be eaten by a tyrannosaurus?

This example leads right back to something we can't stress enough: academic rigor. Your décor must support academic achievement, not detract from it. The decorations are fun, but they certainly won't teach your students what they need to know. If you're waiting for that clever backdrop you made to teach the content, don't hold your breath. But when you can match rigorous content to your theme, the kids get so excited about being in a different space that they're energized from the moment they walk into the room. They're attentive and focused because it's not just another day of being a student at school—they step out of their skin and become a researcher or a surgeon or a spy. They're so engaged with their beach day or moon landing or jungle safari that they don't notice the difficulty of the content.

> **HOPE:** Teachers often tell us they can't do things like a room transformation because they have kids with behavioral issues or learning disabilities. Rather than turning these things into excuses, think of them as roadblocks—and then find a way around them. Once you build up your classroom management by consistently maintaining expectations, even your most challenging students will be drawn into engaging activities. I have a first-grade lesson I call Contraction Surgery that I teach with a room transformation. I set up the room like an operating suite and play a soundtrack of ambient hospital sounds. I meet the kids at the classroom door dressed in a surgical gown and gloves and immediately start speaking to them as if they're my surgical colleagues. (I even hand out surgical masks and caps!) The lesson involves cutting words apart with scissors and then bandaging them together to form contractions. When I did

this as a first-year teacher, my discipline was not on point and I had some problems in the O.R. (Full disclosure: A student snipped off a small lock of her own hair. Trust us, it's not always perfect for us, either. Fortunately, the parents were not upset.) I quickly realized I had to set firm expectations. Once I got those expectations down, I saw amazing results from Contraction Surgery. Let me tell you that story ...

Ryan was one of my most challenging students. He had severe ADD and couldn't pay attention to anything for very long. He knew he was "different," and he'd often cry about it. But it wasn't his fault. Telling him to focus would be like telling a kid with asthma to "breathe easy." When I did Contraction Surgery that year, Ryan was one of the most precise and focused workers. I stayed in character, always talking like a doctor and not a teacher, and Ryan fell into his role as well. I didn't say, "Oops, you have a mistake here"; instead, it was, "Dr. Ryan, can you go back and revisit Patient 14? He's not healing well, and I need a second opinion." On that day, Ryan was not the kid who struggled in class. He was not the kid getting scolded for a behavioral lapse. He was a talented surgeon performing important work. It made all the difference in the world to him.

Kids with learning deficits need engagement the most. They benefit the most. School is hard for them emotionally as well as academically. You have to make them want to be there! By understanding their needs and working to boost engagement, you can create opportunities that allow every student to experience success.

WADE: One of the students I had the hardest time teaching was a boy in my sixth-grade science and social studies classes. Sebastian was mischievous; he liked to talk back, and we were always butting heads. I knew I had to reach him somehow, but I was ready to give up. I finally had to ask myself, *How can I foster a relationship with this child?* Music is one of my biggest engagement strategies, and I already knew this kid was good at drumming because I'd seen him play the *djembe* (a traditional African hand drum—we use them in our classrooms to build energy).

This is actually the point at which I added the full rock 'n' roll drum set to my room. I got a hefty discount on it by playing the teacher card and, once it was in place, I approached Sebastian with a deal: I said, "Okay, I'm going to teach you how to use drumsticks and stay on beat with a metronome; we're going to work on this on Saturdays. And if you apply yourself and do well, you can be my drummer and play drums in class."

So I taught Sebastian the drums. I set the expectation that, in class, he would focus on me and pay attention so he'd know when to drum. And things started to change after that. Our relationship, his classroom behavior, and even the energy in the classroom improved. I'm not going to tell you it was all rainbows and butterflies. I had to be consistent with my expectations for Sebastian even when he messed up. He still acted out and talked back at times, but we were making progress.

I have a lot of songs to help the kids remember content in my current events and ancient civilization classes. Sebastian and I worked together; I'd play guitar and he would keep the beat while the other students sang. There's a strong connection when two people are playing music together. They have to be in sync with and invested in each other. Music changed the dynamic between us, and it gave this kid a reason to want to be in my classroom. It gave him a role to play that was completely different from his mischief-maker role. It empowered him. His behavior improved, and so did his grades. We stayed in touch after he graduated. I'm proud to say Sebastian has become quite the scholar in high school. To this day we have a strong bond. And that drum set and the role of classroom drummer have been part of my classroom environment ever since. A student named Jaydon took over after Sebastian graduated.

These are just a few examples of what we've worked up to after many years. We urge you to try something different with your classroom environment too. Switching things up is a sure way to get your students' attention and make them wonder what you're up to.

Maintain a High Level of *Energy*

In your classroom, you set the trends. You determine the vibe. Your students pick up on your energy from the minute they enter the room—so you want to start on a high note. If you lack focus or purpose in getting the day started, your students will too. When you move at a snail's pace or get distracted by a thousand fussy tasks, you give off a vibe of low energy. Do you want your students meandering slowly to their seats and dawdling with their backpacks and supplies? No, you don't. You want urgency and energy. Which means you have to model it.

Engagement calls for energy, because energy drives effort. You want your mood and the way you greet your students to communicate that what you have to offer today is an electrifying learning experience. You want to strive for high energy, but you also want positive energy—which is not, "Hurry up, come on, you have ten seconds; don't keep me waiting." That may be energetic, but it sounds a lot like scolding or nagging, which is negative energy. We are firm believers that how you start your day is how you will end your day. If you start out with low energy, your students will reflect that right back at you, and you'll all drag each other down.

Both of us like to start the day or the period with a class song. When we taught lower grades, we wrote our lyrics ourselves, but in middle school we generally let the students do the songwriting. The

Wade rocking out with his fifth-grade social studies students

class song isn't content driven; it's motivational, with lyrics about learning and success and rocking it at school. We pick a tune the kids are wild about and already know, something by Justin Bieber or One Direction or whoever is popular at the moment, and then we rewrite the lyrics. Wade plays guitar as the students enter the room. Hope likes to greet students with some version of "Good morning, students! I'm so happy to see you. All right. Get your stuff out. Ten, nine, eight, seven, six, five, four, three, two, one. Here we go, fifth grade!" And the kids bust into that song, and they dance and laugh, and the energy is through the roof. At the end of the song, there's a clapping routine we do and then *BOOM!* They're in their seats and ready to go, starting out smiling and attentive as the lesson starts. This is what high energy looks like! Consider it a small price to pay that you have a Justin Bieber tune stuck in your head for the rest of the day, or that you're butchering all the current hits with your homegrown lyrics.

We both love using music to raise the energy level in the room, but it's only one example of what you can do. The way you open class or start the day is about you, so find something that feels authentic. Singing may not be your game, but maybe a STEM challenge is—especially if you're currently using worksheets for bellwork while you take attendance and get morning tasks out of the way. A STEM activity means students will start the day immediately engaged with a hands-on, inquiry-based activity. They're excited to get into the classroom and solve a challenge through trial and error. Just remember that you have to be ready to start teaching immediately afterward. You'll lose that urgency—and their attention—if you're shuffling through your materials or looking for something you misplaced.

Movement is one of the best ways to maintain energy in the classroom. "Brain breaks" are short movement activities that get the kids on their feet for a minute so they can get the wiggles out. Research indicates that brain breaks improve concentration. It doesn't matter what your brain breaks look like; just find a way to get kids out of their seats and get the blood flowing. Wade plays guitar, and the kids dance during brain breaks. Hope occasionally has a twenty-second "snowball fight" with her class—instead of having the students pass their written work to another student, she lets them wad up their papers and toss them at each other. When the time is up, each student grabs a "snowball" and smooths it out and the lesson continues. You can also teach content with movement. One of our colleagues, Kim Bearden, has a hand gesture for every punctuation mark. We both use competitive games (paired with rigorous academic standards, of course!) that get the students out of their chairs.

We've already mentioned that we put a lot of our content into songs. Music not only brings tremendous energy to the classroom but can serve as a great memory aid for anything our students might struggle to remember—like the emperors of Rome, the process for close reading, steps in the scientific method, or categories of current events. Think about it: Would you rather stand up and sing, or sit through a boring drill of vocabulary and terminology? Kids memorize song lyrics easily, so this is an engagement strategy that lets you work smarter instead of harder. (Hope's first-graders could sing every rap song on the radio, and she couldn't believe what was coming out of their mouths—so she was *really* inspired to rewrite the current hits!) You can often download the karaoke version of a popular song from the web, so you'll have the music without the vocals. If you're way out of your comfort zone writing content-heavy song lyrics to an existing tune, make it an energetic class activity: Let your students vote on the best set of lyrics or combine the best verses to make the whole song. Choose the music your students connect to, whether it's pop, rock, country, or hip-hop. Combining music with movement—dance steps, clapping, arm gestures—raises the energy in the room even more.

That's the lowdown on building energy. The magic starts with you, so go for it! Make it big and make it bold, but do it authentically. *Your high-energy mode doesn't have to look like ours.* We're all very different people, and our classrooms should reflect that. The bottom line is that no matter what you envision for stepping up the energy in your room, you are the only one who can make it happen. Your energy is contagious—so get ready to start an epidemic!

Build a Culture of *Empowerment*

You can empower your students in two ways:

- By building strong relationships with them (and fostering their supportive relationships with one another)

- Through instructional strategies that give them ownership of learning

Relationship building is critical to your creative breakthrough. Trust us, it will be difficult to pull off something like a mock trial or a content-based competitive game until you lay a foundation of trust and mutual respect. The goal is to get to the point where your students sincerely want to work for you and do their best. We're not just talking about your students' respectful behavior toward you as a teacher— we're talking about a true connection and a working relationship that reflects caring, compassion, and concern.

HOPE: The transition to teaching middle school wasn't easy for me. My efforts at engagement initially fell flat, and I had behavioral problems as a result. It was awful, feeling like I didn't have control in my own classroom, and I was a wreck. On one of my worst days, I went to talk to Ron Clark about my problems, and I burst into tears. It was a total

> meltdown—snot, slobber, the whole waterworks. (I can be slightly dramatic from time to time.) I blubbered to Ron that I was going to be Cruella Deville if that's the level of discipline it was going to take to get control. I sobbed that I was going to get those kids to respect me one way or another—and that I didn't care if they disliked me in the process.

Ron is a pretty strict disciplinarian, and at some level I expected he'd agree with me. Instead, he gave me a tissue and a few minutes to compose myself, and then reminded me that, in fact, we *do* want our students to like us. "When was the last time you went out of your way to do something spectacular for someone you didn't like?" he asked me. It was a complete reality check. In that moment, I knew I had to decide if I was going to live in the meltdown or face the problem and beat it. I guess it's not exactly a spoiler if I tell you I eventually got it all worked out.

It is critical that we, as teachers, find ways to form bonds with our students. We all should connect with kids, not just as authority figures but in ways that inspire and encourage them to succeed. This ties right into your classroom culture. In a truly supportive environment, students are invested in each other's success, which boosts every individual's confidence. This drives engagement because confidence is the fuel that makes students want to offer up answers and participate in a discussion. When students actively praise and

Hope with her friend and mentor Ron Clark

celebrate each other for their accomplishments, it raises the energy in the room while fostering a culture of empowerment.

We love to use class cheers to let our students reward and celebrate each other. For example, when a student gives a stellar answer, Hope throws out the cue, "That answer is hot!" and the class celebrates that student by standing up and chanting, "Ice is cold but fire's not; she's FIRE, she's HOT!" Who wouldn't want to be in an environment where everyone is your cheerleader? This is an easy empowerment strategy to implement. Just write your cheer (or find one online), and set your expectations for your class (remembering that it takes twenty-one days for a behavior to become a habit). This simple step can set the foundation for a positive classroom culture, where students share a mutual respect and strive for greatness together. To create the magic, you have to build your village. Everyone has to be on board.

Lessons and activities that foster self-discovery and meaning-ful involvement contribute to both empowerment and engagement. We're especially passionate about creating a learning environment based on inquiry. Whenever possible, we design lesson plans that let students research, experiment, test things out, or use the scientific method to solve problems. We let them role-play in activities like mock trials and Wade's model United Nations activities. This is really where kids learn because they're allowed to indulge their natural curi-osity about things. They become hungry for knowledge and actively pursue it rather than sitting in a classroom while a teacher delivers information. When you turn the tables on your kids and ask *them* to find the answer, it's not only immediate engagement, it's good practice for life.

HOPE: I'm always on the lookout for inquiry-based ideas for my fifth-grade science class. Every now and then, I like to present my students with a task that really has no solution.

Recently I had them do a sink-or-float experiment with candy bars—Snickers, Tootsie Roll, Three Musketeers, you name it. I asked them to determine which types of candy would sink in water and which ones would float, and to record the results. Well, they finished that quickly and looked at me like, *Is this all you've got? What is this, first grade?* Then I told them they had to think like true scientists and figure out how to reverse their results—how to make the sinkers float and the floaters sink based on their knowledge of buoyancy and density. Well, they failed miserably. I saw those faces; the kids were starting to shut down. Honestly, there's not a solution. There are a few things you can do to affect density and buoyancy,

Hope's fifth-grade science students using their inquiry skills, knowledge of physical and chemical properties, and instructions to create their own slime in the Ninja Turtle sewer.

like putting a metal spoon in the water, but I didn't give them a lot of supplies. I wanted to see if they had that grit, that ability to push through and stay motivated and encourage one another. Finally they found a way to get a sinker to float (add salt to the water), and the entire room erupted in cheers. They were jumping up and down in excitement, high-fiving each other, and feeling more motivated to continue their efforts. And they had a good reason to be excited: They actually had to work hard for something. When was the last time you saw a student cheer after finishing a worksheet?

Another inquiry-based lesson was all about making "slime." When I found out that slime was all the rage with my students, it was almost too good to be true. If you've somehow missed this craze, slime is the modern-day equivalent of Play-Doh or Silly Putty. It's a squishy substance with no apparent usefulness but plenty of appeal—kids are not only making it, but trading and selling it as well. I just knew I could tap into that cool factor if I integrated slime-making into a lesson.

In case you don't know, making slime is an exacting process. Every step is crucial toward getting that just-right gooey texture. So in the true spirit of inquiry-based learning, I turned the kids loose to figure this out on their own. Can you guess how that went? Predictably, the students clicked on the first website that came up in their search results. They printed out the instructions, but read no further than the list of ingredients. Then they grabbed those ingredients from the stuff I had available for them and began throwing them all into a bowl. At this point, I fought my instincts to yell, *Stop the madness!* I held my tongue as they combined ingredients in the wrong order and then stirred the goopy mixture instead of kneading it. I let it go because I knew my kids were on the brink of a valuable lesson—one that can only be learned through failure.

Yes, I said it. FAILURE. It's such an important part of the learning process. Ultimately, the students failed spectacularly at slime-making. They quickly found they had created anything but slime. On the other hand, they now completely understood what I meant when I said procedures must be followed exactly. They also learned how to recover from mistakes, figure out which errors they had made, and correct them in the next attempt. And all that learning happened *in addition to* the science content of the lesson! This is the kind of learning environment we could never create with worksheets.

When teachers allow students to fail—and to learn from their mistakes—they teach more than a standardized curriculum; they teach resilience, confidence, and strength. They demonstrate that people don't always win in life and that it's okay. Children need to learn that no one can succeed at every attempt and that it's important to keep working. They need to learn how to gracefully acknowledge the success of others without feeling defeated themselves. We've seen so many teachers go out of their way to reward everyone in the class in an effort to avoid tears or some other form of breakdown. Is this empowerment? Not to our minds. We say embrace the tears. Bring on the breakdowns. Without them we can't instill true confidence and a strong sense of self in students. Educators will never teach kids to be strong, resilient individuals if the goal is to avert every meltdown.

During your students' breakdowns, you cannot live in the present *but must focus on their futures.* Of course you want to take away the sting of a mistake, but the world will never do that for your students.

In fact, the world will just keep throwing sting after sting after sting. Students must learn how to recover and come out victorious in their own battles. This might be the single most important tip we give you in this chapter: *Set firm expectations for the behaviors you want when it comes to recovering from mistakes and celebrating the success of others.*

We don't believe in automatically rewarding every child. Instead, we try to instill enough confidence in our students that they can take risks. Hope has created a reward system she calls "Unlock the Magic," specifically designed to incorporate the elements of chance and risk. The students earn keys for academic and behavioral achievements, but there's a catch. At the end of the quarter, they're invited to try their color-coded keys in the matching padlock—and only one in twelve keys will "unlock the magic" to give that child a spot in a special reward trip. When Hope talks about this activity in our workshops, there are always a few teachers who are horrified that a reward system could end up in disappointment. But we've taught our students the mindset of *Now is not my time, but the next time might be—and meanwhile, we're going to celebrate those students who did unlock the magic and will be going on the outing.* It goes back to those expectations. We set the bar pretty high with this activity, but our students are able to stretch and hit that level because we have empowered them to do so.

Empowerment may seem like the most overwhelming of the four *E*s, so we'll give you a strategy to start with, one that doesn't cost anything: *Get into the mindset that you're not teaching a classroom but rather the individuals in the room.* As soon as you adopt this way of thinking, you'll naturally start noticing each student's distinct personality and strengths.

> **WADE:** One of the ways I lift up my students is by writing short, personalized notes to each one. They're really simple and don't take much time—just a few lines on an index card

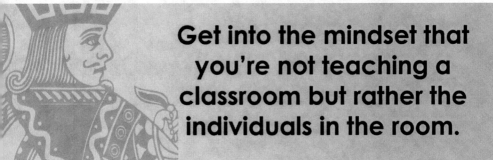

Get into the mindset that you're not teaching a classroom but rather the individuals in the room.

or a piece of note paper. I'll mention a strength I've noticed, something I see them doing in school, what they bring to the classroom, or how proud I am of something specific they've done. I always try to visualize my students as young adults, so I bring in that aspect as well to let them know I can see them being successful in life.

I love your interest in technology, and I can see you working in the tech field someday.

You brought such positive energy to our history discussion yesterday, and it really helped the group to focus.

I've noticed your talent with writing. I hope you'll keep exploring and developing that talent after graduation.

The notes are all different because my goal is to show these kids that I see them—truly see them as individuals, separate from their classmates. I never thought about the impact this could make until I found out that one student, Christopher, had set my note on his bookshelf at home and read it every day until his eighth-grade graduation. It's empowering for kids when someone believes in them. As teachers, we have that power—and we shouldn't forget to use it.

Wrapping It All Together

We've already mentioned that teachers ask us all the time how we do it. They ask us this because they've formed the impression we pull off something spectacular every day, either a room transformation or science experiment or a game or a new song. But if we did a room transformation every day, it would lose its magic. If all we ever did was sing songs, the appeal would disappear. If students played Word Sneak in Hope's classroom in the morning and then played it again in Wade's class that afternoon, we'd see kids tuning out.

Predictable will never equal magical. The truth is, what people see on social media or our blog is a highlight reel. There are many days we walk into our classrooms, and all we have is our teaching. That's our reality, just as it is yours. It's impossible to have something special for every single minute in the classroom. And when all we have is our teaching, it has to be darn good. It has to be high energy, and it has to be compelling. There are ways to build engagement through instruction just through your delivery—your voice, your movements, and the strategies you employ to keep all eyes on you.

Predictable will never equal magical.

There's an expression in show business: *Always leave them wanting more.* You don't want to exhaust your repertoire or pull out every trick you have or leave your audience entirely satisfied. You want to leave them wondering what you'll do next so they'll be eager to show up again tomorrow.

We have to dare to be ourselves, however frightening or strange that self may prove to be.

—May Sarton

CHAPTER EIGHT

Authenticity

**Identify your go-to thing
and start there.**

A re you ready for some good news? Here's the scoop: As an educator on a creative path, you have an amazing—but long overlooked—resource right at your fingertips. It's your secret weapon in the war against classroom boredom. It's your sorcerer's stone *and* your ruby slippers all rolled into one. It's that ace up your sleeve that will transform your hand and magically stack every deck in your favor. Stay tuned; we're about to show you how to play that ace strategically.

But first let's back up a bit.

We are fortunate to work at a school where every one of our colleagues is a master educator. Yet all of them are doing their own thing. Each has a teaching style that is completely different from the others. They all bring an individual talent or special interest into their classrooms. They could never switch roles or swap teaching styles *because each one is drawing on his or her authentic self in a manner that drives engagement.* The result? As our students change classes throughout their day, each period brings a different experience and a different environment. Our kids can't help being stimulated, challenged, and engaged.

That ace up your sleeve is what we think of as your "go-to thing." It's something you love to do or something you're good at. It might be a talent, skill, hobby, or just an interest you want to indulge. It can be anything you dabble in or spend time doing outside of the classroom. And it's going to be your starting point as you try out different ways to build student engagement and deliver content more creatively. As you progress with your creative breakthrough, your go-to thing will be the point at which your personal interest meets your professional mission of engagement.

We had an elementary school colleague, Mary, who loved gardening. Her classroom was a cheerful place, with African violets blooming on the windowsill and philodendron vines trailing down the side of her desk. She had no trouble pairing her content with her passion.

Her students germinated bean seeds into edible sprouts. They fed tiny bits of hamburger to a Venus flytrap. Every year for St. Patrick's Day, they would dye white carnations green by putting the stems in a vase of water and food coloring to see how plants absorb water. They even studied the life cycle of butterflies by watching it happen right in front of their eyes: They saw the eggs hatch, watched the caterpillars grow fat on milkweed leaves before spinning their bodies into a chrysalis, and finally witnessed the mature butterflies emerge. The unit ended with a field trip to release them in a community butterfly garden. Mary's students had many fun learning experiences under a gifted educator who knew how to apply her love of all things green and growing to elementary education.

Gardening is not a standard. Yet Mary was able to pull it into her lessons in all sorts of ways. And why not? Educators can link gardening to many different standards at all grade levels, including standards that deal with textual evidence, scientific inquiry, life cycles, characteristics of organisms, ecosystems, natural resources, environmental issues, biodiversity, adaptions of organisms, and heritable traits—remember, Gregor Mendel worked with pea plants to discover the rules of genetic inheritance through dominant or recessive traits. But why limit yourself to science? It was crop failure that led to the Irish potato famine, which started a historic wave of immigration—and immigration is a social studies standard.

Your go-to thing—whatever it is—holds tremendous value. Working in your own element allows you to be passionate about *how* you teach, even at those times when you're not wild about what you're teaching. It increases your sense of personal fulfillment and gives you a more positive work-life balance. When you bring your go-to thing into the classroom, you spontaneously become more creative because you're connecting the dots between who you are as a person and who you are as a teacher. You're living authentically, being true to your own spirit and celebrating your innate gifts. In his memoir, novelist Stephen King (no relation to us!) shrugged off criticism of his niche in the horror genre, saying, "I was built with a love of the night and the unquiet coffin … It's what I have." Let's *all* keep it that real. Let's all work with what we have. Authenticity is a huge part of creativity.

> *WADE:* When I was in tenth grade—and not a brilliant student, by a long shot—I joined up with some friends to form a Christian band called Thorns of Glory. I learned how to play guitar, how to load a van like a roadie, and how to hook up the amps and speakers—but I also learned how to put individual talents to work for the group and how to be a leader. And I discovered how important it is to be around good people with common interests and goals. Your vibe is your tribe.
>
> I spent several years with the band, driving around and playing music. I couldn't have gotten through college without those guys; they were my family. And I had no idea at the time, but that experience was my foundation for using music in the classroom. Looking back, I can see how it really cemented the idea that music is a powerful way to reach people, to make connections. I'm not even a super-talented musician. I love playing an instrument, so I do it for my own enjoyment. In my second year of teaching, I was reflecting on who I was as a person and who I wanted to be as a teacher. And that's when

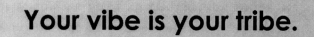

Your vibe is your tribe.

Wade and his bandmates (from left to right): Wade King, Nick Cullen, Will Forrest, Travis Jeffcoat, Grant Reeves

Wade drumming with his students at the Ron Clark Academy

I got the idea to bring my guitar into the classroom and write content-based songs. I thought I would enjoy doing that, and I hoped the kids would enjoy it too. I started playing songs I liked by Michael Bublé, and my students didn't really know who that was, but they got to see who I am.

I think you have to be true to who you are. Today, most of my students are into hip-hop music. So it's a give-and-take situation because I'm still using pop and rock music in the classroom, but we're learning from one another. Your classroom should always include elements that are authentic to you because your students will notice that. They'll see that you're not just trying to conform or fit in somewhere.

HOPE: I was raised by a mom who is so creative, craftsy, and capable that I swear she can turn poop into gold. She was an accountant turned stay-at-home mom, so she looked for ways to earn money with her creativity: She decorated wedding cakes. She threw painting parties. She hung wallpaper in people's homes. She started an embellished sock business with a friend—yes, really! I had a perfectly matched pair of painted socks for every outfit I owned. We lived up to our ears in paint and yarn and beads and craft supplies, even though my mom kept our house immaculate. On any given Sunday, I could look over at my dad in church and find a speck of glitter on his chin or in his ear. I guess that's what he gets for marrying a creative genius!

When I needed something to keep me busy as a kid, my mom put a smock on me and sat me down with a project of my own, right at her side. I'd have my own little cake to decorate or my own pair of socks to paint. Crafting with my mom shaped me as I was growing up. It's why I'm so passionate about hands-on learning. My mom always had that make-it-work mentality. If she had to fix something or design something, she'd just figure it out. So I grew up with tactile learning. I mastered the higher-level thinking that comes from being given basic materials and expected to create something from them. Basically my mom was using STEAM to teach me at home, before STEAM was the cool thing to do. This allowed me to explore, make mistakes, and get messy—sometimes *really* messy. Hands-on learning allowed me to develop confidence and my own make-it-work mentality. I was never afraid to dive headfirst into brand-new things.

Hope and her students in her Poetry Picnic room transformation at the Ron Clark Academy

The pastors at our church were also exceptionally creative, and this influenced me as well. I can vividly remember the way they brought lessons to life. (I loved it, although sometimes they—and my dad—would wear costumes that absolutely terrified me when I was really young.) Pastor Ray once turned the entire youth room into the belly of a whale to teach the story of Jonah. (Of course, my mom was on hand to help.) They covered the entire room—floor, ceiling, walls—in black plastic. Then they tossed green beans, sliced bananas, gummy worms, and canned spinach all across the floor to mimic the contents of the whale's stomach—it was a little slippery, to say the least! They set the mood with dripping sounds, which my mom made with a keyboard. (YouTube wasn't a thing yet.) The lights were off, and all of us kids were blindfolded as we entered the "belly" to hear our pastor teach the lesson. I remember every detail: every sight, sound, and smell. And because of that, I've never forgotten the story of Jonah.

Another time, the children's pastor, Pastor Mark, simulated the experience of a missionary trip for all of us kids. It was an elaborate transformation of the entire children's ministry facility. We walked into the "airport" and immediately went through security to board the "plane." Upon arrival at the "Honduras Airport," we went through "customs" and had the experience of "customs officers" choosing certain "missionaries" to have their bags ransacked and searched. Once we were out of the airport and into the country of Honduras (the main building), we tasted the local foods, experienced the music and culture, and learned about the sacrifices missionaries make to do their important work. And today, this memory is so clear in my mind that it's like it all happened

Hope's mother, Pam, visiting Hope's first-grade class as Aunt Suzzy Adjective for their descriptive writing lesson

yesterday. Why? Because it was a true learning experience, one that plunged me into a different world.

Fast forward to my college years, and my mom and I took over the children's ministry. This was the perfect opportunity for me to try out my wildest ideas. We did it up big, just like my pastors did for me. A year later I became a teacher, and room transformations naturally became my go-to thing.

What's *your* go-to thing? Maybe you already know exactly what it is. But if not, let your mind go back to the reflection part of this process. Do you remember those eight distinctive learning styles we all learned in our college education classes? They're a great starting point for reflecting on your interests and how they might relate to creative classroom activities. We've made some connections for you between the intellect types and interests they correspond with. Do any of these speak to you as your go-to thing?

Visual-Spatial—physical space, architecture, model-building, carpentry, maps, navigation, geography, jigsaw puzzles, origami, photography, illustration, cartoons, comic books, film and video, graphic design, fashion design, interior design, landscape design, home improvement projects

 Bodily-Kinesthetic—dance, movement, hiking, jogging, exercise, making things, crafting, acting, role-playing, pantomime, charades, rock-climbing, yoga, gymnastics, skateboarding, rollerblading, cycling, sports, juggling, health and medicine

 Musical—sound effects, rhythm, listening to music, attending concerts, writing lyrics, composing songs, playing an instrument, speaking rhythmically, rapping, opera, musical theater

 Interpersonal-Social—interacting with others, discussion groups, debates, seminars, dialogue, letter writing, travel, cultural studies, politics, etiquette, community service, social media, team sports, competition, clubs, genealogy, holiday traditions, entertaining

 Intrapersonal—self-reflection, meditation, scrapbooking, keeping a journal, reading, writing poetry

 Linguistic-Verbal—reading aloud, word games, writing, poetry jam, stories, essays, listening to the spoken word, humor, giving speeches and presentations, podcasts

Logical-Mathematical—thinking conceptually or abstractly, solving puzzles or mysteries, law, philosophy, carpentry, quilt-making, computer science, programming, chess, strategy-based games, astronomy, engineering, experiments, scientific method, crime investigation, forensics

Naturalistic—gardening, pets, wildlife, bird watching, weather, geology, farming, agriculture, collecting specimens, terrariums, fishing, SCUBA diving, insects, reptiles, ecosystems, life cycles, food chains, biodiversity, ecology, natural resources, climate change

Maybe you have hobbies or interests we haven't thought of or that don't fit neatly into one of these intellect types—anything you're interested in can become your starting point.

Getting Started

How do you connect the dots between your go-to thing and your content? We both got started using our go-to things—music for Wade, crafting for Hope—in the classroom very naturally without thinking about it too much. It was trial and error for us, and it will be for you too. You'll need to just jump in, but we can outline a general process for you to experiment with.

Choose a Theme

When you're planning a creative lesson, *choose your theme first and then figure out how to integrate it with content you need to teach.* This is important. We've learned it works best this way rather than doing it the other way around (starting with the content and trying to pin it to a theme). We don't have an explanation for why this is true, other than this method taps into personal passions. We find that if we're really excited about our theme first, the rest just falls into place.

Your theme can be anything that calls to you. We've been inspired by movies, books, sports, video games, even late-night TV. The idea is to pick something you love and would like to bring into the classroom. In this example, let's say it's October, and you want to do something that's kooky and spooky (even if your district won't let you say the word *Halloween*). You love vampire stories, so you decide on a vampire theme as your first step.

Determine the Content

Next, you look at the content and standards you need to teach. What can you relate to vampires, considering the grade level and subjects you cover? Let your mind go wild here. What can you come up with? Potential content ideas might include blood types (life science), folklore and myths (reading comprehension), understanding cultural differences (social studies), or day length and seasons (physical science)—because, of course, vampires must avoid the sunlight.

Plan the Lesson

Once you have your theme and your content, the last step is to figure out what the lesson itself will look like. This depends on the boundaries of your comfort zone—how far will you go? You can play it safe and rely on Halloween decorations from the dollar store to bring your theme to life. You can live it crazy by dressing up as a vampire. You can go all out and create a whole new lesson plan (or special activity or game) with tons of elements from vampire mythology. Or you can adapt an existing lesson, activity, or game to incorporate your theme in some small way: vampire trashketball, anyone?

That's the process, in a nutshell. The tricky part is getting that balance between content and creative delivery. As you experiment with creative delivery methods, remember to strive for academic rigor.

We can't stress it enough: The extra stuff you bring into your lesson to drive engagement must support the lesson, not distract from it. The bottom line is that your students have to learn the content and retain it.

When you're new at this, stick with content you know inside-out and sideways. Don't go all out on an elaborate activity if you're teaching an unfamiliar unit. There's a good reason for this warning: When you're confident about the content, you won't waste time if the extra stuff fails. If your students can't figure out the clues you wrote for your scavenger hunt, or if the circus tent in your room transformation collapses (believe us, we've been there!), you can roll up your sleeves and teach the content with nothing but your smile, your passion, and your enthusiasm. You won't have lost a day of teaching. If something flops and you can't quickly modify the activity, try to make that failure into a teachable moment. Exactly what was wrong with those scavenger hunt clues? Can you analyze them together as a class and work backwards to rewrite them? Can you show your students the value of trial and error as opposed to always striving for perfection? As Thomas Edison said, "I haven't failed. I've just found 10,000 ways that didn't work."

Whenever you introduce something new to your students, *you have to sell it*. It could be a morning chant, song lyrics to reinforce a history lesson, or a competitive game to drill math skills before a test. Whatever it is, be excited about it! Remember, if you're not selling it with enthusiasm, your students aren't buying.

WADE: Some of my favorite chants and cheers come from movie lines. If I see something on the screen that I love, I automatically want to bring it into the classroom. But before I introduce the new thing—let's say it's a call and response—I'm going to play that movie clip for my students. And I'm going to die laughing while it's playing. (Jimmy Fallon does this. He's the master of exaggerated laughter because he knows laughter is contagious.) I want the kids to think that clip is the coolest and funniest thing they've seen all week. I want them to assign value to it. And they might not be as passionate about it as I am at first, but it doesn't matter. After a while they own it and think it's the greatest thing ever. I did this with a hilarious line delivered by Jack Black in the movie *Nacho Libre.* When the kids in the orphanage got in trouble for tussling with each other, he defended them by saying, "They are just *niños* trying to release their wiggles." (Okay, you have to actually *hear* it to think it's hilarious.) So now when my students get fidgety or restless, I call out, *"Niños!"* and they respond with, "Wiggles!" while they shake their shoulders. We release the wiggles, and then we all get back to work.

When I decided to do a lesson based on the Power Rangers, I really had to sell it. That was something I'd grown up with:

Jason David Frank, aka Tommy from the original Mighty Morphin' Power Rangers, helped create a magical moment for the students. Pictured from left to right: Hope, Jason David Frank, Wade

The movie version of *The Mighty Morphin Power Rangers* was released back in 1995. I had to introduce my students to the Rangers before I sprang my lesson on them so it would have meaning for them. I brought in video clips from Netflix and gave them some background information. The special effects in that movie are crude by today's standards, so we talked about how much technology has changed in the past twenty years. I sold it as nostalgia. I sold it as an authentic film experience before this era of sophisticated digital effects. It was a way to show them why they should be interested. And it worked! In the lesson that followed, I made comparisons between U.S. drones in the Middle East and the mechanical "zords" in the movie. Hope did a close reading with the kids, using biographies of the film's actors. And we held a debate on whether or not the alien enemies in the film were entitled to human rights protections if captured. The bottom line is, if you act like something is the coolest thing ever, you sell it through the intensity of your interest.

Selling the magic is easy to do in the early childhood grades because little kids have an innate sense of wonder and awe. By the middle and high school levels, a lot of teachers feel self-conscious about introducing anything outside the ordinary. They're likely to say they already know their eleventh-graders won't respond well to games or songs—but it's because they feel awkward themselves. If you feel uncomfortable going into it, and you let that awkwardness show, your students will respond awkwardly. Just step boldly out of your comfort zone and do it! You'll be surprised by how well your students respond. And if your new idea really does flop somehow, just move on. You can either modify it for next time or think of something completely different.

Occasionally when you do something new in the classroom, you'll catch one or more students rolling their eyes, snickering, or otherwise reacting to something they find cheesy or corny. Just ignore it. Just do *you*. Muster the confidence to carry on. Boys of a certain age, in particular, feel compelled to act like they're above it all or too macho to participate. It doesn't matter what they're showing you on the outside; the important thing is what's happening inside—and we guarantee you they're loving all your wild and unpredictable engagement strategies. What's more, they're actually learning.

> **HOPE:** I'll never forget Mrs. Boyd, my ninth-grade geometry teacher. I remember her teaching positive slope and negative slope with hand motions and a song. We'd all march around the classroom like a train, making an equal sign with our hands and singing the song. Was it corny? You bet it was. But it was fun, and everyone got into it—including the burly football players. Geometry can be a tough subject, but Mrs. Boyd was confident enough to teach it in a way that worked. And it *really* worked, because I remember the song to this day: "Parallel lines have equal slopes; perpendicular—negative reciprocal." My memories of Mrs. Boyd are so clear. I remember her face and her joy as she led us in that song and march. I remember how her smile completely illuminated what was, in my mind, a dull subject. It spoke volumes.
>
> Have you ever had a teacher who did that for you? Don't you want to be *that* kind of teacher for your current students? As educators, our mission is to change kids' lives. And to do that, you have to give them something that will stick forever—even if your students want to act too cool for school. Just pick up your pride and move it to the side, I say. Our WHY is not about what our students think of us. Not long

ago I was talking to a group of kids after school, and I used an expression they thought was outdated. One of them said, "Mrs. King, you know people don't say that anymore." I just smiled and told him, "Well I do, and that makes it cool!" Kids appreciate that. When you model authenticity for them, you show them it's okay to be who you are.

Leveling Up

One of the best things about your go-to thing is that it helps you aim for engagement activities that have real-world applications. If you're teaching fractions to third-graders, your kids don't realize yet how often they'll use that skill in everyday life. But if your go-to thing is cooking or baking, you might teach fractions with pizza slices or through doubling and halving a brownie recipe. Once again, baking is not a standard. Yet you can create a learning experience by linking kitchen skills to standards like fractions, decimals, measurements, following a procedural text (i.e., recipe), chemical reactions, and scientific inquiry. When we were student teaching, we did a whole cooking unit with science and some basic math. Even kindergarteners can make lemonade.

When you base an activity on your go-to thing, and you have good results, you can then build on your efforts. *If you have something that works, expand on it*! Don't make more work for yourself by starting from scratch with something new. Let's say you did a fraction lesson with pizza slices. Leveling up might look something like this:

- The next time you do a math lesson based on food or cooking, you pull in multiple math skills or perhaps add a writing or science component to teach across content.

- You expand the lesson further by giving your students an opportunity to create menus—perhaps linking the prices to an exercise with decimals and asking the students to use descriptive writing skills to make each menu item sound appealing.

- When you're really confident about pairing your math content with your food theme, you have your students create a budget for a virtual restaurant. Maybe they'll have to price menu items by calculating the cost of the ingredients from a supply list you give them.

- Finally, a room transformation really takes it to another level. You set the mood at your pizzeria with red checkered tablecloths on the desks, an Italian dinner music playlist from Spotify, white aprons for the "wait staff," and the specials of the day listed on your whiteboard.

Can you see yet how this might work with your own content and go-to thing?

How fast you level up depends on your personality, how much you're willing to risk, the level of trust you have in your students, your classroom management skills, and how confident you are in the content and your ability to maintain that academic rigor. Keep the Rules of Rigor in mind and remember that you can maximize your success by working smarter rather than harder when you're planning special activities.

Avoid the Comparison Trap

It's almost inevitable. As soon as you begin to find your stride along the creative path, the Joker will put up a tripwire. In an effort to make you fall flat on your face, he'll point out every wonderful thing that other teachers are doing while he whispers in your ear that you don't measure up. Don't listen to the Joker! Don't fall into the comparison trap! You sabotage yourself when you start comparing your efforts to anyone else's. Instead, celebrate every baby step you take. If you stepped out of your comfort zone to try something—anything—different, consider that a success. If you wrote content-heavy song lyrics, that's a success too—even if they don't rhyme as well as Ed Sheeran's. If you transformed your room into an Italian restaurant with nothing but plastic tablecloths and background music, tell yourself you rocked it. And never, ever, *ever* compare your starting point to someone else's end point. As soon as you start thinking, *Oh I want to teach just like Mr. Smithers down the hall,* you've thrown authenticity out the window. You're trying to build on what someone else has already done, but you haven't laid the groundwork to get there.

Comparison will steal your joy, every single time. We know because we've been there. We both started teaching at RCA and promptly forgot how to be ourselves. We lost our identities because we were trying to teach just like all the brilliant educators around us. It's funny because we are two totally different people, but we both fell into the trap of trying to stuff ourselves into someone else's mold. Wade didn't bring his guitar into the classroom until November that year, even though he'd used it when he taught his model lesson for RCA administrators during the hiring process. We made ourselves very unhappy by comparing ourselves to and emulating people who had talents that weren't our talents.

Ultimately, we both found ownership in ourselves again. Through reflection, we figured out we were harming ourselves and letting our students down. We realized we'd been hired for what we could bring to the table, but then cheated everyone by failing to show up with anything new. We had to tell ourselves, *I'm just going to be me, and it's scary because I don't know who they expect me to be or what they will think of me, but I'm going to own it.* Once we did that, everything fell into place. It will for you too.

When you stop comparing yourself to others and only measure yourself *against yourself,* that's when you start improving. When you embrace who you really are, authenticity becomes your platform. Instead of emulating someone else, you adapt an idea to fit you. You use your individual strengths and talents to set the stage and play to that sold-out crowd. It's not selfish to focus on developing the talents that are authentic to you. Your students are going to feed off your energy and your enthusiasm, and if you're passionate about something, they're going to own that too.

> **WADE:** In our workshops, I talk to teachers about the value of their strengths and talents. And, as usual, I use a sports analogy to get my point across. (Hey, that's what I do!)
>
> I start out by asking my audience to think about Shaquille O'Neal and Dwight Howard.
>
> "What are they known for?" I ask.
>
> People call out the most obvious answer, "They're basketball players."
>
> "Okay, what else are they known for?"
>
> Now the answers get more specific. "Dunking points in the paint." "Defense!" "Rebounds."
>
> "Oh my goodness, what a long list of athletic talents! Do you think they're aware of those strengths?" I ask.
>
> Everyone responds, "Yes!" because, of course, they're aware.
>
> Then I tell the group there is one other thing that Shaq and Dwight are known for—and everyone is stumped. Finally, I pull up a slide of these star athletes shooting free throws. And I say, "These two individuals make millions—*millions!*—of

dollars playing basketball, yet you and I could probably do better than the one out of ten free throws they make."

Everyone laughs because they know it's true.

"Do you think they know how horrible they are at free throws?" I ask.

Everyone laughs again and nods. Absolutely, they know it. "Hack a Shaq" is a coined phrase that means to intentionally foul a lousy free-throw shooter to gain an advantage.

So what's my point?

Both of these men show up at practice and work on their free throws—but not nearly as hard as they work on their dunking, rebounds, or defense. They *know* they're terrible at free throws and can only improve just so much. So they concentrate on their natural talents and what they enjoy doing. That's what makes them star basketball players.

Do you want to be a star educator? Focus on your natural talents and the things you love. That will lead to professional growth and success. Shaq wouldn't—and shouldn't—try to be a three-point shooter. You shouldn't try to be something you're not, either.

Ideas Everywhere!

Being creative doesn't mean you have to constantly come up with new ideas. Let's face it: There are probably no new ideas in teaching. We borrow ideas constantly from other teachers and anything that calls to us. Our eyes are always open, looking for something we can adapt for the classroom. We were once on a cruise ship that held a game night, and we saw people playing a giant game of Simon Swipe. It's a memorization game with flashing colored lights, and we just turned and looked at each other and thought the same thing—our students would love this!

There are ideas everywhere. When you see someone doing something you want to try, it's better to "steal" that idea than to copy it. When you grab an idea and run with it, your efforts are authentic to you. That's called inspiration. But when you set out to duplicate something or emulate someone exactly, that's just an attempt to hijack another person's success. It's like putting on clothes that don't fit you because you admired them on someone else. As film director Jean-Luc Godard said, "It's not where you take things from; it's where you take them to."

WADE: People automatically associate me with music. Visitors to the school actually think I'm the music teacher! But there are other things I love as well, and I bring them into the classroom whenever I can.

I'm a complete news junkie, and I follow politics closely. So it makes sense that I teach a current events class, but I've also brought my passion for politics into my eighth-grade science class. When I taught science content about renewable energy, I structured the lesson as a town-hall-style debate. I created the mock city of Kingsville, and assigned various roles to all the students. I made it real for them by allowing them to dress for their parts instead of wearing their uniforms that day. Some of the kids represented energy companies who were coming to Kingsville City Hall to pitch their particular energy source (solar, nuclear, etc.) to the town. The rest of the students were the town citizens who had to think like stakeholders and question the energy companies about the pros and cons of each option. Every single student was involved during the simulation. That's important for academic rigor. We never plan a debate that leaves any students on the sidelines.

It was a fun way for me to teach science content using politics as my go-to thing that day. It also offered inquiry-based learning for the kids as they researched and prepared for their roles.

I also love superhero movies, so that's another one of my go-to things. When Hope planned a room transformation with the Teenage Mutant Ninja Turtles as a theme, I jumped on board with a lesson about feudal Japan for my ancient civilization class. And I got so excited about the movie *Captain America: Civil War* that I saw it in the theater three times. It was right up my alley because the United Nations figured into the plot, and I teach a unit on how World War II led to dissolving the League of Nations as a forum for resolving international disputes in favor of the much stronger United

Mariah, one of Wade and Hope's students, participating in a Model United Nations conference in Hamburg, Germany

Nations. Naturally, I made superheroes the theme of that unit that year.

And who doesn't love Jimmy Fallon? I think he's hilarious! He has a segment I love where he competes against his guests in silly games. One of them is Egg Russian Roulette, and it's hysterical. There are a dozen eggs. Some are hard

Wade's seventh-grade students enjoying a rigorous game of Social Studies Egg Russian Roulette

boiled and some are raw, and the players take turns choosing one and smashing it against their foreheads. As soon as I saw that, I knew I was going to use that idea—kids love a disgusting mess. I decided to use Egg Russian Roulette in a review instead of playing Jeopardy as usual. That morning I was setting up and cooking eggs on a hotplate I borrowed from the science lab, and the kids could tell something was going on in my room. They came to class excited, anticipating a surprise. And they loved Egg Russian Roulette! The kids answered review questions the same way they would in Jeopardy, but I added the rule that every time an individual player got six points, he could choose someone from the other team to "play roulette" with an egg. Basically, I tricked them into going through the review questions faster because they really wanted to see someone smash a raw egg on his face—and they had to have six correct answers before that could happen. There was a lot of positive energy in the classroom that day!

If these examples don't show you that *anything* can be your go-to thing, then we don't know what will! We mean it when we say you can pull your go-to thing from any type of interest at all, including your favorite movies, TV shows, or sports.

Hope has a whole unit based on NASCAR racing. She teaches the science standards of force and motion through a series of activities that include constructing balloon cars and a Lego derby. The lesson, based on inquiry, allows the students to test the effects of friction on "test tracks" made of various materials like sandpaper and tinfoil. To bring in language arts, she has the kids research a real NASCAR driver and his statistics, then write a persuasive essay to pitch that driver and team to potential NASCAR sponsors. If car racing is your thing

Hope's fifth-grade science class testing their LEGO cars on the friction track

too, you could use these ideas or develop lessons about aerodynamics, alternate fuels, or math problems involving speed and distance. You could create a morning song or a call and response with a "start your engines" theme. You could even bring the car-and-racing theme into your classroom décor.

If you love true crime stories and TV shows like *Law and Order*, a mock trial is a terrific instructional strategy that you can adapt for any grade level. Just tie the theme to your content, and teach your students the format of the trial in a way that's suitable for their age. The goal is not to imitate reality but to create a learning experience that allows students to analyze and evaluate information, develop listening skills, and gain confidence with public speaking.

We've used mock trials very successfully to bring literature to life. At the middle school level, we've used Harry Potter books, which our students can't get enough of. We put Rubeus Hagrid, the groundskeeper at the Hogwarts School, on trial for negligence in his handling of the sorcerer's stone. Our students had to rely on their understanding of the story's plot line to identify likely witnesses and piece together the evidence. Each played a role: judge, attorneys for defense and prosecution, witnesses, and jury.

At the high school level, you could stage a mock trial using pretty much anything your students are reading in literature. At the elementary level, you could start with a fairy tale, such as *Goldilocks and the*

Hope and Wade's sixth-grade ELA and social studies students participating in a Harry Potter Mock Trial

Three Bears. There are many versions of the story, so you'd have to choose one, read it together as a class, then discuss it before staging a simplified mock trial. If students aren't old enough to improvise a trial effectively, you could work from a prepared script. Did Goldilocks break the law when she entered the home of the bears? Did she steal from them when she ate their food?

Once you've built stronger relationships with your students and learned more about them, it might feel authentic to you to work with *their* interests instead of your own. This way you choose something that's all the rage with them right now—a book, movie, video game, or song—and learn something about it, then plan a lesson around it; for example, if you find your kids are into social media, you might have them summarize a text in 140-character tweets or put together a Snapchat story based on a historical figure. At the time we were working on this book, our students were obsessed with fidget spinners, and we were looking for a way to use them with our content. You really can't go wrong with incorporating students' interests into your lessons. In doing so, you're tapping into the brilliant minds of toy companies, game designers, musicians, animators, and popular food brands. They have the time and money to create the things kids go nuts over—so let's piggyback on their efforts and adapt them for the academic world.

These are just a few random examples to get you thinking—so don't stop here! If every teacher in every school was drawing on an authentic interest somehow, we'd have exceptionally well-rounded students. Kids really benefit from that exposure to different settings, teaching styles, and content delivery methods. So be yourself, always. But be your best wacky version of yourself.

The block of granite, which was an obstacle in the pathway of the weak, became a stepping-stone in the pathway of the strong.

—Thomas Carlyle

CHAPTER NINE

Grit

**Push through barriers and
overcome obstacles.**

Just reading through this book to the end is not going to make you a creative genius. You truly must have an intention and a purpose, and you must *practice* being creative. We've aimed for a book that will challenge you, because a challenge requires action, and action leads to change—but it doesn't happen overnight. It's a lot like resolving to spend time at the gym to get the abs you want. As much as you'd love to spend one morning pumping a little iron, and (*Boom!*) have a beach body just like that, the reality is very different. You can sit down and dream about that perfect physique, or you can make it happen. In life, you get the choice to either dwell in your fantasies or pursue your vision in reality. We truly believe the best things in life are worth working for. And that means not only putting in the time and practice, but waiting long enough to see the work pay off.

Your creative path is a process and a journey, and that means there are roadblocks and obstacles along the way. Unlike a fitness journey, however, this one allows for plenty of chicken wings and hot fudge sundaes! So break out the ice-cream and don't bother with the bowl—consider it fuel for this next leg of your journey as you get ready to grow your grit and tackle those obstacles!

Just as your creativity will look different from ours, so will your roadblocks. In fact, even though we're a married couple, best friends, and colleagues who work side by side, we have faced very different challenges along the road to our creative breakthroughs. You might breeze right through an obstacle that one of us has struggled with, because your background and talents have equipped you to do so. Other obstacles are going to take tenacity. You'll have to find your way under, over, or around them.

The barriers along your creative path fall into two main categories: systemic and personal.

Systemic barriers include all those frustrating teacher problems that pop up in today's education system and make you want to repetitively bang your head on your desk. We get it because we've been there. Your list might include any of these things or others we haven't included:

- Budget constraints
- Standardized testing
- Scripted curriculum or standards
- Unsupportive administrators
- Parents' expectations
- Burned-out colleagues
- Unmanageable class size

On the other hand, personal barriers include all of those "life gets in the way" kinds of things. No one is perfect, and everyone has individual struggles. Both of us are introverts, and neither of us is really a morning person—that's a struggle right there. We start our mornings in completely different ways. Hope will say out loud every thought in her head. She'll ramble off a list of everything we have to do that day … or month … or year. Wade likes morning quiet time to reflect privately about his day. It takes a full cup of coffee before he can formulate a sentence. We ride in to work together in the morning, and sometimes we're at odds or we get into an argument. (Can you imagine commuting with your spouse every single day? Let the good *and* bad times roll, right?) Regardless what happens in the car, we have to find a way to overcome it because we can't take our problems into the classroom with us. We can't let personal struggles become an excuse to lose our enthusiasm or a day of instruction time.

Remember way back in Chapter Two when we talked about getting into a no-excuses mindset? An excuse is a defense mechanism. It's a justification for giving up. It's a falsehood the Joker plants in your mind to make you believe you can't do something. The Joker doesn't want you to leap over hurdles—or even to sneak under them. He'd really like to stop you dead in your tracks. If you listen to the Joker and start coming up with excuses for why you can't do something, you'll never be able to create magic in your classroom. The magic only happens when you shift into no-excuses mode and focus on the path in front of you—roadblocks and all.

We've faced many of the same challenges in education that you have. We've had those days when we felt like we could barely keep our heads above water. And we've learned that the most frustrating things we faced as teachers—district mandates, never enough money, scripted curriculums—were obstacles we could handle if we set our minds to it. You can get past your obstacles too. It may not be easy, but if you face those hurdles now, you'll find triumph just down the road in the form of engaged students.

Crush Your Curriculum Challenges

We've said it before, and we'll say it again: Life—and teaching—are all about the way you play the cards you're dealt. No one can stack the deck against a smile, passion, enthusiasm, and desire. No district superintendent or school administrator is going to say you can't do those four things. Your classroom is your stage—how are you going to use it?

Many teachers view curriculum as a set of scripted standards that suck the joy out of teaching. Maybe you feel this way too. Maybe you go into school every day, and you feel like you don't even want to be there because you hate the curriculum. Well, if you hate that curriculum, your kids will hate it more. If your curriculum is a teaching barrier for you, it will become a learning barrier for your students. Why be a barrier when you could be the wild card? Just muster up that grit and look at your curriculum as a roadblock with a detour just waiting to be discovered. Start small, change just one thing at a time, and experiment with creative ways to deliver that content. We promise you, it gets easier as you build momentum!

Why be a barrier when you could be the wild card?

WADE: I was a terrible math student all through my school years. Math never came easily to me. Well, when I moved from Townville Elementary to Pendleton, I was assigned to teach every math class at the fifth-grade level. Goodness knows that was the last thing I wanted! At the same time, I knew I had to suck it up. I had to show up and teach math to fifth-graders who were still struggling with fourth-grade math skills.

This is the year I started bringing my guitar to school, writing songs, playing competitive games, and experimenting with ways to drive engagement. My students loved the Disney Channel, so I tuned in regularly to learn about their interests (I even sat through dozens of episodes of *Hannah Montana* with a notepad on my lap). I looked for anything I could connect to math skills, and I found plenty to work with. In class we played Human Battleship to learn about plotting ordered pairs. We sang songs to master elapsed time and types of triangles. I even rewrote the lyrics to Bruno Mars'

"Billionaire" and played guitar while we all sang *I wanna name my triangles, oh so bad. Right, obtuse, acute is what I have ...*

At testing time, we had some of the highest scores in the state of South Carolina, with 94 percent of the entire fifth grade—including the resource students—scoring "met" or "exemplary" in grade-level performance. This didn't happen because I was good at math. It was all about the way I presented the content. I knew what those kids needed because I had been a struggling math student myself. I taught in a way that let them really home in on the concepts that I couldn't grasp at their age. I did this every year and always outscored everybody in the district.

HOPE: Sometimes it's easy to have enthusiasm for your content, and sometimes it's not. One year I had a week to teach thirty-six Greek and Latin roots. Insert all the huffs, puffs, moans, and groans ... from *me!* I absolutely hate teaching vocabulary. And to be honest, most students don't like it much either (although a few are wordies; vocabulary is like a puzzle for them, and they enjoy figuring it out.) I wanted to find a way to make it fun, because I knew this was one of those concepts I would have to trick them into learning.

To make the lesson come to life, I turned my classroom into a giant game of Twister. I took all the desks and chairs out of my room, printed the Greek and Latin roots on colorful paper, and used double-sided tape to stick them to the floor. I would spin the wheel and say something like, "Right hand, empty!" and the students would find the prefix or suffix that matched the clue. (Of course, I incorporated the Rules of Rigor from Chapter Eight. Remember: no turns, no outs, and

Hope's fifth-grade students playing Greek and Latin Root Twister

every student answers every question. The students who fell would move to the sidelines, where they would write their answers on a Frisbee with a dry-erase marker.)

I also had the kids take a Greek or a Latin root and turn it into a superhero. If the prefix was "aqua," they could morph it into Aquaman. Then they had to write a riddle and come up with an appropriate costume for their hero. As a result they had a visual image of all the Greek and Latin roots that stuck with them in a way that pure memorization could not. It might have been easier to hand them a worksheet and say, "Okay, I've covered that standard," but that would not have created a moment the students would remember.

Never stop for obstacles that exist only in your mind. Over and over again, we get the same comment from teachers who've seen one of our creative lessons or activities recapped on YouTube or our blog: *I wish my administrator would let me do something like that.* We're not sympathetic to that statement. If you've said something similar, we challenge you to reflect on whether it's truly grounded in reality—because we think you'll find it's an excuse. It's often just a little too easy to point the finger at someone else. Ask yourself if you are actively working on (1) flexing your creative muscle and (2) earning the respect of your principal by showing results.

One of the reasons we keep saying "start small" is so you can practice pairing your creative delivery method with academic rigor. *You have to show that what you're doing right now actually **works** before you can take it to the next level.* If your test scores are in the dumps and you attempt a fancy room transformation, of course your principal is going to think that kind of activity is fluff!

Your reality may be that you have to spend a year busting your butt and laying the groundwork for your efforts. By that we mean supporting your principal (and that includes not gossiping or complaining behind the admin's back) and working with your class in ways that let you demonstrate results—also known as rising test scores. If your admin is okay with songs and music in the classroom, start there and write those lyrics to make your content memorable. If your admin is okay with games, make that your key strategy for reviews. (Just don't forget those Rules of Rigor.) Prove yourself with academics. Once you can show results, you're likely to gain your admin's support.

Trounce Those Testing Troubles

Back in Chapter Six, we asked you to reflect on your attitudes toward standardized testing. So many teachers view these tests as an obstacle and say they spend too much time reviewing for them. Others object to being evaluated on the way their students perform. But since you're now working within a no-excuses mindset, you can view standardized testing as a challenge—rather than something that defines you, defines your students, or dominates your classroom culture. How will you meet that challenge? With engagement, of course!

If you're cramming in a huge review the week before each test, naturally you're going to be stressed. (And you'll probably pass that stress on to your students.) But if you use your time wisely during the year and get your students engaged to the point where you can teach quickly and rigorously, those nerve-racking, last-minute reviews become a thing of the past.

> *HOPE:* Remember my story about turning my classroom into a beach to give my students a sensory experience? That room transformation took place three days before our standardized test at the year's end. I'm not kidding. I removed all the chairs and tables from the room. I had a blue tarp on the floor for the ocean and a tan painter's cloth for the beach.

Hope's stress-free classroom in South Carolina right before state testing

I had pails of sand. I had low beach chairs and umbrellas, colorful towels, pinwheels, beach balls, and posters of palm trees. I had beach sound effects and cheerful beachy music playing. I even gave each child a lei to wear. And a few of my colleagues thought I had lost my mind! They were stressing and reviewing like crazy, handing out packets of worksheets for every skill and concept they had taught that year. Meanwhile my students spent their "beach day" rotating through various review stations, spending fifteen minutes at each one. They were quiet, engaged little worker bees. They weren't stressed, because I wasn't stressed. I had spent the whole year preparing my students for the upcoming test rather than trying to cram it all into a few days at the zero hour. My students retained the knowledge they'd acquired throughout the year because they had experienced learning as a series of memorable moments (at testing time, 96 percent of them met all criteria in every single content area). That's the power of engagement.

WADE: I was an athlete in high school and college, and that competitive mindset has carried over to the way I view teaching. I look at the school year as if it's training for that big championship game. Every class and every lesson is a workout. It's practice. And practice should always be harder and more rigorous than the game itself. When game day comes, it's a celebration. It's marching bands, cheerleaders, and "We Are the Champions" playing over the loudspeaker. That's how I want my students to feel about test day. So I talk it up; I sell it. I tell them, "This is where you get to go out there and kick some butt." We've sung all our content songs together before the test. I've even showed them video clips of Ray Lewis and Muhammad Ali. One of our principals in South Carolina, Dr. Black, really exemplified that game-day mindset about testing. He'd have people from the community come into the school and line the hallways; they'd be cheering and high-fiving our students as they filed into the room where we were testing. It really pumped up the kids and let them feel pride in their accomplishments. Mindset matters. It plays a huge role in student achievement. As teachers, we should all model that winning mindset.

Mindset matters.

If you find yourself saying things like, "Oh, those low test scores are just because of this group of kids I have this year," it's probably time to go back and really reflect on your teaching that year. Were you giving 100 percent? Were your students giving 100 percent? Did they really *want* to learn? As a teacher, you're like a track-and-field coach. You prepare your students as best you can and then turn that race over to them, hoping they cross the finish line without leaving anything on the track. When you have this mentality about required assessments, you not only stretch yourself, you're likely to find that your test scores—and your students—will grow beyond your expectations.

Bust Through Budget Boundaries

More often than not, people assume we have a huge budget to finance our creative efforts or that our school reimburses us for expenses. Nothing could be further from the truth! We are blessed to have supportive administrators who would give us the world if they could. But money doesn't grow on trees. Like you and all the other teachers in America, we pay for our supplies out of pocket. Remember the game of Egg Russian Roulette from Chapter Eight? Wade bought those eggs on his way to school in the morning. That rock 'n' roll drum set in his classroom? He first came up with the idea to use drums as an engagement strategy, then he hit the pavement until he found a pre-owned set and someone willing to give him a huge discount. Hope's room transformations are always done on the cheap. She'll beg, borrow, and prowl the aisles of dollar stores and thrift stores until someone tells her it's closing time.

Don't use money as an excuse. Accept the challenge. Never limit yourself. Look for ways to make "the impossible" become reality. You'll be happy you did, and your creativity will flourish. It's okay to cut corners, because the kids do not notice small imperfections, nor do they deem anything as lacking. You will never hear a student say, "This room transformation would be so much better if …" If you do something different, *that's* what kids will notice.

Accept the challenge.
Never limit yourself.
Look for ways to make
"the impossible"
become reality.

HOPE: Call me crazy, but I refuse to let a little thing like money determine how I'm going to teach! I did a room transformation called The Chemist's Carnival that people assumed was wildly expensive, but it really required very little cash and a lot of advance planning. (I call this concept *making it happen*.) It was a science lesson about observing and identifying physical and chemical changes. I had students doing scientific research at five separate stations: a cotton candy machine, a snow cone maker, a popcorn popper, and a funnel cake fryer—*all borrowed for the afternoon.* (Needless to say, my students' minds were blown when they arrived at class.) There's nothing to stop you from using my little beg-or-borrow trick. You'll be surprised what you can get just by asking.

Hope's fifth-grade science class set up as a Chemist's Carnival

Hope's fifth-grade students tasting their way through the Chemist's Carnival

I did purchase some of the materials (like red-and-white-striped table skirts) that I used to decorate my classroom in a carnival theme. These came from a party supply store, but in general I do a lot of my shopping at thrift stores and Dollar Tree. And remember, I've been doing these transformations for ten years, so I've built up quite a few resources—bins and bins of resources! From time to time, I buy a more expensive item if it's something I can store and use for other lessons and room transformations; for example, I bought a pricey roll of artificial turf that I use several times a year, so the investment was worth it.

I also want to point out that my earliest room transformations were not nearly as detailed as they are today—yet my students' excitement was no less than it is now. Back at Pendleton, I transported my third-graders to "Lucky's Punctuation Patty-O" with nothing but green plastic tablecloths and some hand-lettered signs. I made them believe that a little leprechaun had paid us a visit to make sure our punctuation skills were on point, and they were completely engaged.

It really doesn't take much to get started, so just do *something!* If you have a great idea, come up with the minimum supply list you need and figure out a way to get those things. Check your closets and ask your neighbors and friends if they have any of the things you need. Post your wish list on social media. If you have a friend who's a graphic artist, ask for help making signs, game cards, posters, etc. Work the phone and call local businesses. Explain your project and ask for materials to be lent or donated. You'll find that many people will be all in when it comes to helping you make magic for your students.

Work Through Personal Struggles with Self-Awareness

It's much harder for us to give you strategies for your personal roadblocks, because everyone reading this book is going to have a different kind of struggle. Systemic roadblocks are almost always excuses, but that's not the case with your personal issues, because you are who you are. You can't go back and change your past, and in many cases, you can't change your innate personality traits. We mentioned before that we're both introverts; that has an influence on everything we do. But we're not even the same kind of introvert—one of us is far more outgoing and social than the other. We could go on for days about our inner struggles, about how one of us lacks confidence at times, about how one of us is disorganized, about the way laundry piles up so high at our house that the only way to get caught up is by doing sixteen loads at once in a laundromat.

In Chapter Eight we talked about not comparing your creative efforts to anyone else's. The same holds true for your personality and your soul. As writer Anne Lamott put it, "Never compare your insides to everyone else's outsides." You may be watching someone and thinking they have it all pulled together, when in reality that person feels broken and scared and is working hard to fake it till she makes it.

> **HOPE:** I've always felt the need to excel at everything. I'd try to be the perfect teacher, the perfect friend, the perfect daughter, the perfect business woman, the perfect wife. People would even make comments to me about my "perfect life." What they don't know is that my unrealistic expectations for myself came with a huge price tag: I struggle with panic attacks. On many days I am perfectly fine. On other days I'm crippled with panic.

It took me a long time to connect the panic attacks to my perfectionism. Since then I've had to realize I am never going to be perfect, and that is okay. I'll never be the perfect teacher. Those shiny Instagram posts? Highlight reel! Just keepin' it real! I'll never be the perfect wife. Y'all, I can't even boil water. I'll never be the perfect friend. I have 265 unanswered text messages on my phone as I sit here and type. But what I've learned is that life is not about being perfect. It's about how you deal with your imperfections. It's about how you handle those internal struggles and those external roadblocks. Now I just strive to be a better person than I was yesterday. That's realistic. That's growth. That's healthy. I've learned that if I am not taking care of *me*, I can't possibly be the best teacher for my students. So if your struggle is similar to mine, step away from the idea of perfection. Embrace the idea of growth instead.

On the creative path, comparing yourself to others can lead to jealousy or perfectionism where it didn't exist before—and both are destructive to creative roadblocks. In *The Artist's Way*, Julia Cameron advises that perfectionism is not about getting something right; it's a refusal to let yourself advance. She writes, "Perfectionism is not a quest for the best. It is a pursuit of the worst in ourselves, the part that tells us nothing we do will ever be good enough—and that we should try again." If you struggle with perfectionism, ask yourself who will benefit from your obsession with perfection. We've already noted that kids don't care if your lesson materials are perfect; they don't even notice. If you get hung up on perfecting the details, you'll never become a master of the unexpected.

It's the same with jealousy. You might look down the hall and see what another teacher is doing and feel that first jealous pang. If you don't nip it in the bud right there, jealousy will derail your creative efforts. Cameron writes that jealousy is a mask for fear. When you feel jealous of another teacher, ask yourself if it's because you see that person doing something you're not brave enough to attempt. Remember that you have a different path, one that is authentic to you. Then summon up your grit and try something new.

And then there are those times when courage or confidence is in short supply. When you're stretching yourself and trying something new, it's natural to have the jitters. It's like walking through a haunted house at Halloween time—you're not afraid of the ghouls, because you know they're just people in costumes. The "fear" comes from anticipating what's around that corner and wondering whether or not it's going to grab you. It's a fear of the unknown. When you try new things in your classroom, it's the same thing. You're going to be on edge and jittery because it's something new, and you don't know what to expect. But once you've experienced those jitters two or three times, you get to a place where you expect those feelings and just accept them as part of the creative process.

> **WADE:** I always told my athletes that feeling nervous was a sign of dedication. That anxiety means you're giving it your all. If you didn't care about your performance, you wouldn't be nervous about it. I always had butterflies in my stomach before a wrestling match. And honestly, I get a little nervous before I teach *any* lesson at school, Monday through Friday. Those are thirty human beings I'm having an impact on every single day. When I start speaking, it's like I'm holding their lives in my hands. I'm shaping their futures. I'm educating the leaders of tomorrow. I think if you don't feel just a tiny bit nervous about teaching a plain old lesson, you're not reflecting

on how important your job is. You should always have those butterflies, a little bit.

What's *your* biggest roadblock? How will you get past it? As we said in Chapter Six, it can take a lot of reflection to map out your path. If you can be honest with yourself about your obstacles and your struggles, that's the first step toward improvement. Your roadblocks are things you can manage with the right kind of effort. Stick with it! Keep moving forward. But don't forget to stop occasionally and take a minute to enjoy the view. You're on the road to making magic. You're on the path to becoming the wild card.

You are always a student, never a master.
You have to keep moving forward.

—Conrad Hall

CHAPTER TEN

Persistence

Persist with and build on your creative efforts.

A dam Peterson is a passionate educator who teaches kinder-garten in Illinois. Like us, he teaches in the same school as his spouse, has an active social media presence, and is on a never-ending quest for engagement. He's always played acoustic guitar in his class-room, but after a visit to Wade's classroom in Atlanta, Adam decided to take things up a notch. In his vlog, Adam enthusiastically explained how he had looked around Wade's *School of Rock* themed room and felt inspired. He realized he had a lot of similar equipment at home including speakers, an amp, and music-activated LED lights, and it was one of those lightbulb moments—you know the kind we mean!—when an idea took hold and wouldn't leave. "When I'm not deejaying or when I'm not playing, those things just sit in my garage," Adam said. "Why? I've paid so much money for those things, why are they just sitting in my garage?"

It's not hard to guess what happened next. Adam moved a lot of his deejay equipment into his classroom and set up an amp and speakers. Then he plugged in his guitar. "And honestly, my acoustic guitar always gets the kids up and moving and motivated, and they have so much fun," he related on his vlog. "But plugging it in and run-ning it through the speakers was like playing a brand-new instrument in here. They absolutely loved it!" As if that statement needed proof, Adam switched to a clip of his young students having a little dance break. The bass was booming, the colored lights were flashing to the music, and everyone was in motion.

Do you see what Adam did there? He created magic. He switched up just a couple of little things and created a whole new experience for his students. But more importantly, he found a way to build on his creative efforts and expand on his go-to thing by using music and his guitar in a different way.

Creativity is not a plateau. It's not a destination you reach and settle into. *If you ever start to feel comfortable, it's a sign you've stopped growing.* This statement may be corny, but's it true. We know this from firsthand experience.

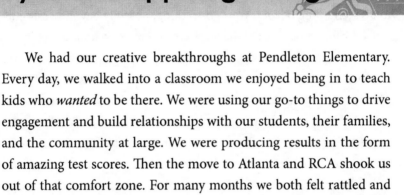

If you ever start to feel comfortable, it's a sign you've stopped growing.

We had our creative breakthroughs at Pendleton Elementary. Every day, we walked into a classroom we enjoyed being in to teach kids who *wanted* to be there. We were using our go-to things to drive engagement and build relationships with our students, their families, and the community at large. We were producing results in the form of amazing test scores. Then the move to Atlanta and RCA shook us out of that comfort zone. For many months we both felt rattled and unsure of ourselves. We struggled with new obstacles and new challenges. And ultimately, looking back from where we stand today, that was a time of tremendous professional and personal growth. That's when we really learned how to take engagement to the next level.

Try Something Beyond Your Go-To Thing

Once you've experienced a creative breakthrough, you'll need to keep stretching and growing because your class will change every year. Not just because it's a different set of students, but because the things that influence kids—media, technology, pop culture—are constantly changing and evolving. You won't necessarily be able to do the same thing over and over again and get the same results. You'll always have to keep one toe outside your comfort zone and push the limits a little. At times, you may feel like you're starting over every year.

The easiest way to defy stagnation is to build on your previous efforts. We talked a bit about this in Chapter Seven, how to take a creative lesson plan to the next level by adding new components and teaching across content. It's always a good bet to start with something that was a success and then make it bigger and bolder. But at some point—you'll know instinctively when you're ready—it will be time to do something beyond your go-to thing, possibly beyond your current comfort zone. We tell the teachers in our workshops to get in the habit of looking around constantly and appraising everything they see in terms of *How could I use this in the classroom to drive engagement?* This is how Adam Peterson thought to add an amp and music-activated lights to the way he currently uses music. It's how Wade got the idea for Egg Russian Roulette while watching late-night TV. And it's how Hope knew that making slime could bring her science lesson to life. When you're using your powers of observation with a long creative lens, you'll find inspiration in unexpected places.

As you draw on your own talents and interests, make an effort to learn about the talents and interests of others. What are your colleagues doing that you could tap into? Is there someone with whom you could partner? Music might never be your go-to thing, but it's hard to avoid it, really, because the kids love it. You don't have to sing or walk around with a guitar in order to write lyrics to an existing tune. You might not be the star of the song, but that's okay. The point is not to be the best at something, but how to make it work for you.

Start a Club

Your opportunities to grow as an educator don't necessarily have to relate to academic content. Extracurricular activities can be a great way to build relationships and flex your creative muscle. Back at Pendleton Elementary, we found that we couldn't limit ourselves to the students in our classes if we wanted to make the whole school a magical learning environment. We looked for ways to reach out to more students and give them a purpose to come to school every day. But it even went beyond that. So many of our students were latchkey kids who didn't have a purpose *after* school either! They were getting into trouble too often, and we'd hear about kids being suspended or even expelled. So we started after-school programs two days a week to give them something positive to do.

WADE: At Pendleton, the boys were very athletic, and they loved to fight. They were always getting into fights on the bus, and that turned into one of our biggest behavioral problems. So I said, "Okay, you want to fight? I'm going to teach you a respectable way of fighting." With that, I started a wrestling program at the elementary level. Wrestling is another one of my go-to things. I was never tall enough to have a shot at basketball, so I wrestled all through college. I also served as the high school wrestling coach for our district while I was teaching at Pendleton. Fortunately, the district was supportive, and I got all the permissions I needed to start a new athletic program. And when the kids heard there was going to be a wrestling club after school, you would've thought they'd won the lottery. It was crazy how excited they were. It was a voluntary program, free of charge, and it was completely packed. I got some high school wrestlers to help out with things like moving the heavy wrestling mats, and they were happy to be involved—so that was another set of kids who found a purpose in this little after-school club.

HOPE: I was about two steps behind Wade in forming an after-school club at Pendleton. I thought, *Okay, what are my girls into?* Well, they loved to dance. By the kindergarten level, they were twerking and grinding and using the most inappropriate moves you could think of because that's what had been modeled for them. But I looked at it and thought, *If this is what drives their passion, let's bring it into the learning environment.* Sometimes you have to be *very* creative to help kids find their purpose. So I started a girls' step team—even though I couldn't step, couldn't even dance. I got on YouTube and taught myself the basics of stepping, then reached out to a friend who had stepped in college, and she came and volunteered her time.

I presented the step club as something fun to do after school, but both Wade and I wanted our efforts to be about more than having fun. The stepping program lasted ninety minutes after school, but for the first twenty minutes I'd teach etiquette and soft skills like eye contact during a conversation, how to speak politely, how to be respectful. We even practiced table place settings because they didn't learn that at home. And Wade did something similar with the boys ...

WADE: ... but it wasn't really etiquette; it was more on a manly level. I wanted to show them how to be respectable young men, how to step up and help out, how to open doors for people, even what to do when you have a flat tire. We would literally see young boys opening doors at the school for the ladies. We told the kids that the purpose of these clubs and these teams was to uplift the whole school. And it ended up being one of the most powerful things at Pendleton. We no longer saw those kids getting into fights on the bus or getting suspended.

Hope's Girls' Step Club
(second- through sixth-graders)

HOPE: I could walk through the halls and look into a classroom window, and if one of my step-team girls saw me peeking in, she'd immediately sit up straighter and become conscious of what she was doing. They were accountable to me because I'd given them a reason to be. I'd built that relationship with them. And, more importantly, they were finding their purpose and a sense of belonging. They were finding a reason to take pride in their school. This is when I started to realize the difference between a classroom teacher and a *school teacher*—someone who can spread the magic beyond the four walls of a single room.

WADE: We're still helping kids find a purpose at school. That's what my classroom drummer is all about—building a relationship and giving that child a reason to be in my classroom. I'm also giving music lessons after school to a handful of students. I practically have my own school of rock! The kids and I play together on Fridays when we have visiting educators coming in for professional development. It's become a huge component of our school culture, just like the after-school clubs at Pendleton.

Our little experiment with the after-school clubs had a happy ending, one that rippled out into the community. When we first started teaching at Pendleton, there wasn't much parental involvement. We had low turnout for parents' night and very little engagement through our school's Facebook page. Then we got the idea to hold an event highlighting our afterschool clubs' athletic activities. We planned it for a Friday evening and decided the boys would have a wrestling match, with our girls' step team performing a few routines midway through the program. On the night of the event, our elementary school gym was packed with a standing-room-only crowd. The parents of our school may have been uncertain about where they fit into their kids' academic lives, but they sure were passionate about sports in this community, just down the road from the Clemson Tigers' football stadium. And once we got them engaged through their kids'

Wade's wrestling club consisted of boys (second- through sixth-graders) and involved local high school athletes as mentors.

athletic programs, we were able to encourage more of them to turn out for academic nights as well. The parents had also found their purpose and a reason to become involved with the school—so much so that the elementary athletic clubs continued even after we left South Carolina. The annual evening event moved to the much larger high school gym in order to accommodate the hundreds of parents and family members who would show up to support the kids.

This is the power of building relationships: The more links you can add to your chain, the stronger the chain becomes.

Lift Up Your Colleagues

Making magic takes a village. The larger you can make your village, the more magic you can create. It's great to start with your classroom, building relationships with and between your students. Those relationships are the foundation of your engagement activities. But you can also go beyond those classroom walls and include your teaching colleagues in your village.

Find ways to show your colleagues they matter to you personally as well as professionally. Strengthening those relationships can be as easy as remembering to ask about their families or their pets and showing an interest in them as people. Better yet, make a pact with yourself that you're going to perform random act of kindness for a different colleague every month. Take over lunchroom or playground duty. Drop off a healthy snack. Find things to compliment. Stock the breakroom with bottled water.

Go back to the concept of a smile, passion, and enthusiasm. Are you doing these things—smiling, acting on your passion, and showing enthusiasm—consistently with your colleagues as well as your students? It can be easy at the beginning of the year when everyone is excited and motivated, but what about the middle of the year when teachers are exhausted or tired of winter? If you can find ways to lift up your colleagues and avoid some of the negativity that we all know exists in education, that's another creative way to drive engagement. Teamwork makes the dream work.

As creativity gets easier for you, look for ways to give someone else a hand up. Invite another teacher to partner with you and co-teach a lesson together, or lend materials you've made to a colleague. We invited our science teacher, Daniel Thompson, to use a room we'd transformed as a *Super Mario* video game, and he loved it! He taught his seventh-grade science content there when we weren't using the room. He has no plans to try a room transformation of his own, but now he loves helping us set up for them.

Sometimes the best way to get others on board is to ask them for help. The reality may be that you don't need assistance at all, but when you ask for help, you give others a sense of purpose. They get a little taste of what you're doing, their interest is piqued, and before long they have a sense of ownership in your creative project. They see

Daniel and Wade having a little fun while setting up the Super Mario Bros. room transformation

the value, and they develop a sense of belonging. Remember what we said about adding links to your chain to strengthen it? No one wants to feel like the weakest link. Lifting up your colleagues is about teamwork and coming together as educators to create a culture of support for the kids.

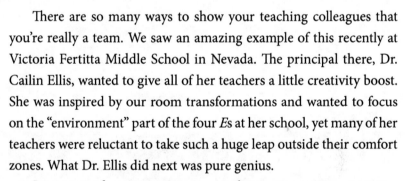

When you ask for help, you give others a sense of purpose.

There are so many ways to show your teaching colleagues that you're really a team. We saw an amazing example of this recently at Victoria Fertitta Middle School in Nevada. The principal there, Dr. Cailin Ellis, wanted to give all of her teachers a little creativity boost. She was inspired by our room transformations and wanted to focus on the "environment" part of the four *E*s at her school, yet many of her teachers were reluctant to take such a huge leap outside their comfort zones. What Dr. Ellis did next was pure genius.

Room transformations are among the most engaging strategies out there to make history, science, and ELA come alive. The outcomes are very positive, yet the setup can be intimidating at first. Dr. Ellis knew this, so she transformed three unused classrooms in her school—permanently. She expertly duplicated our *Jurassic World* room transformation and then created her own plans for two other themes, Alice in Wonderland and Hogwarts (Harry Potter). They are all magical. Now every teacher in the school has access to these extraordinary learning environments. They can all create magic without the effort of setting up and tearing down the set and the props.

Dr. Ellis even held a professional development day where she did a model lesson to help teachers get an idea of how they might use the new settings.

Encouraging the success of others will never dampen your own success. As leadership coach John C. Maxwell said, "Leaders become great, not because of their power, but because of their ability to empower others." Once you find your own creative power, share it. Spread the magic. Don't focus on who's getting credit for an idea. Imagine what education could become if we all worked together and supported each other like Dr. Ellis supported her teachers. We wouldn't just be saying we want to change the world; we would *be* the change.

"Leaders become great, not because of their power, but because of their ability to empower others."

CHAPTER ELEVEN
Snappy Wrap-Up

*I'm talking about living a life that is driven
more strongly by curiosity than by fear.*

—Elizabeth Gilbert, *Big Magic*

One of the things we learned about writing a book is that we're supposed to have a conclusion at the end. That didn't feel authentic to us. It seemed more like something we'd have in a research paper than in a book about creativity. So we decided our go-to thing here would be a short and snappy wrap-up.

Here's a quick chapter review, by number:

1. Be the wild card.
2. If you argue for your limitations, you get to keep them.
3. Don't listen to the Joker.
4. Always know your WHY.
5. These things are free: a smile, passion, and enthusiasm.

6. Lunchtime is a creative opportunity.
7. Make them *want* to come to class.
8. Just do *you.*
9. Don't stop for roadblocks.
10. Spread the magic.

Your classroom is your stage. Each and every day, you get to decide exactly how you will use it. Will your curtain rise to a sold-out crowd and a full house? (In cards, there are 3,744 possible combinations that can make up a full house. So many possibilities … so many ways to use creativity in your classroom to build your audience and sell the magic.)

Be the teacher who fills your students with curiosity and excitement. Make them want an encore. Give them a reason to never forget. Live it crazy and be the wild card that changes the game for them.

Here's our final piece of advice: Find creative ways to build relationships with your students—but don't wear sandals to a cow show. That's a story that will have to wait for our next book … because (wink) the idea is to always leave them wanting more.

PART III
Toolbox

However beautiful the strategy, you should occasionally look at the results.

—Sir Winston Churchill

It's not enough to be industrious; so are the ants. The question is, what are you industrious about?

—Henry David Thoreau

We've already said that life is like a game of cards in many ways. Your circumstances as a teacher are often beyond your control. It's the luck of the draw; it's a randomly dealt hand. Yet, despite the element of chance, a card game also includes *strategy*. And so does teaching. No matter what kind of hand you currently hold—weak or strong— you should be in it to win it. These instructional strategies can help you boost engagement, reach your struggling learners, and challenge more advanced students. They can help you make your classroom a vibrant place to be. They can help your students retain knowledge because they're applying it to hands-on learning experiences instead of memorizing it for the test.

Don't forget, consistency is the key to making something work for you!

Cheers and Chants/ Call and Response

What It Is

Essentially, this is "audience participation" with your students. It breaks the monotony and keeps them attentive and on their toes because they know they have to listen for cues and be part of something.

If you're not already doing these, it's a great place to start your creative efforts—once you have the smile-passion-enthusiasm down.

Purpose

- Help students remember content.
- Build motivation. (Celebrate success, raise the energy in the room.)
- Start the day with urgency.
- Bring students' attention and focus back to you (classroom management).
- Build a positive classroom culture.

Hope and her fifth-graders talking about the content with energy and enthusiasm

Tips

- Don't spend a lot of time teaching them. Introduce it, practice once or twice, move on.

- Model the level of enthusiasm, volume, etc. you want and set that expectation.

- Find them online, write your own, or have the kids write them.

- With a call and response to bring attention back to you, set the expectation that the response includes not just reciting the words, but sitting up straight with nothing in hand, eyes on speaker, and freeze for three seconds.

- Try to minimize dead air. After a cheer/chant/call/response, be ready to start teaching immediately.

Relationships and Culture

What It Is

Building relationships and learning about the culture of your students and the community you teach in is all about knowing them and their interests. This is more effective than assuming your students will adapt to who you are. The idea is to know your students outside the four walls of the school.

Purpose

You, as a teacher, can obtain essential background information about your students' interests so you can make your content relevant and exciting for them. Kids can't build on knowledge they don't have.

Wade's former fifth-grade students are now seniors
in high school in South Carolina.

Tips

- Sit with your students at lunch. Play with them at recess. Accept invitations to attend their birthday parties, Little League games, etc.

- Have students do a "passion project." This allows them to share what they are excited about. It is easy to integrate ELA and Social Studies curriculum with this. Note that this goes far beyond show-and-tell. We had a student whose dream was to be a weatherman, and we never knew this until he did a project on meteorology.

- See geniushour.com for free resources. Genius Hour is a movement that allows students to explore their own passions and encourages creativity in the classroom.

- Regardless of what grade you teach, watch the TV shows your students enjoy. Read the books they like. Listen to their music.

- Remember that your goal is always to lift your students up— even when you have to redirect them.

- Give your students opportunities to learn how to empower each other and lift each other up.

Soft Skills

What It Is

Social skills and other non-academic skills (e.g., handshake, eye contact, how to greet and address someone, etiquette and manners).

Purpose

- Teach beyond the content to prepare students for life.

- Build a culture of respect in the classroom and school environment.

Tips

- Always model the behaviors you set expectations for. Make MAGIC!

- M.A.G.I.C. for students:

    Make eye contact. (All eyes!)

    Accept failure and learn from mistakes.

    Get off your seat—stand to answer questions.

    There is no "**I**" in team.

    Celebrate and empower others.

- M.A.G.I.C. for teachers:

    Make eye contact.

    Add a smile.

    Get your hands up.

    Ignite the passion.

    Command the classroom (don't teach to the board).

Movement

What It Is

Adding physical activities to regular class time. Research confirms that movement facilitates learning (possibly through increased oxygen to the brain). Think of it as a way to *involve* children in the learning process rather than teaching *at* them.

Purpose

- Give kids a break from sitting still (brain breaks).

- Help students to remember content. (Associate hand motions with parts of speech, geometry concepts, etc.)

- Build motivation or attention/focus (combine with a cheer, chant, or call and response).

- Reduce behavioral problems with kids who have a hard time sitting still.

Tips

- Add movement to anything and everything possible—definitely to cheers, chants, and call and response.

- Use hand motions or gestures to help students remember a series of steps or anything else that is hard to grasp. We've come up with motions for each step in the scientific method.

- Games are a way to add movement to a question-and-answer exercise.

Music

What It Is

It's music! It's a shared cultural experience and a universal language. Music has the power to reach people on social, emotional, intellectual, and spiritual levels.

Purpose

- Help kids to remember content (by writing content-heavy song lyrics).

- Create an engaging environment (background music).

- Provide a brain break (combine with movement: drumming or clapping, for example).

- Build relationships with students. (See the "classroom drummer" anecdote in Chapter Seven: Engagement.)
- Use music to create a certain mood in other activities. Think of the famous musical interlude that accompanies the final Jeopardy round while contestants are thinking and coming up with an answer.

Tips

- Popular songs are often available in a karaoke version without vocals so you can sing along with your own version of the lyrics.
- Don't fall into the trap of thinking music is just for little kids.
- Find out what kinds of music your students like and start there, whether country, rock, hip-hop, or whatever.
- If you write song lyrics, don't teach the whole song at once. Each verse can relate to a specific area of your content and can serve as a memory jog as you move forward with the content. If students are struggling with a task, you can remind them of the lyrics and lines that relate to it.
- Don't overdo it or have a song for everything, or it will lose that magical appeal. Save it for difficult content, terminology, or anything with procedural steps.
- Have students sing a relevant content-based song to avoid having dead air while you prepare for your next activity.

Games / Competition

What It Is

A way to make questions and answers more engaging than a worksheet. We often think of our classroom games as a "worksheet on steroids."

Purpose

- Create a memorable learning experience for unpopular or difficult topics.
- Use for test review.

Tips

- Work smarter, not harder: Reserve the use of games for difficult or boring topics or for test review.
- Have good classroom management in place before introducing a game, and keep the game moving—don't allow too much unstructured time.
- Remember the Rules of Rigor:
    - No one waits to take a turn.
    - No one strikes out and sits on the sidelines.
    - Every student answers every question.

Current Events

What It Is

A structured way to teach from the news, including politics and policy, global concerns, etc. Current Events is not a tested content area; however, the skills involved with Current Events align well with some ELA and Social Studies standards.

Purpose

- Develop informed citizens and lifelong newsreaders.

- Educate our students on how to become global citizens and leaders.

Tips

- Teach your students why a news story that makes headlines is important.

- Don't steer clear of current events because you don't know how to integrate them. Use a news story as a text for reading comprehension or link it to a history topic.

- Make sure students understand why something is news. Have them look at the front-page headlines of a local paper and talk about why each story made the headlines. Reasons might include the following:

  - *Timeliness*—News that is happening right now, news of interest to readers right now

  - *Relevance*—The story happened nearby or is about a concern of local interest

  - *Magnitude*—The story is great in size or number; for example, a tornado that destroys a couple houses might not make the news, but a story about a tornado that devastates a community would be very newsworthy

- **Unexpectedness**—Something unusual or something that occurs without warning

- **Impact**—News that will affect a large number of readers

- **Reference** to someone famous or important—news about a prominent person or personality

- **Oddity**—A unique or unusual situation

- **Conflict**—A major struggle in the news

- **Reference to Something Negative**—Bad news often "sells" better than good news

- **Continuity**—A follow-up or continuation to a story that has been in the news or is familiar

- **Emotions**—Emotions (e.g., fear, jealousy, love, or hate) increase interest in a story

- **Progress**—News of new hope, new achievement, new improvements

Debate

What It Is

A structured discussion about a specific topic. It can be used to discuss literature, history, even how to solve a math or science problem.

Purpose

- Develop critical thinking skills. (Students have to research facts to formulate an argument.)

- Provide a memorable learning experience.

- Develop an understanding of different perspectives, including the difference between opinion and fact.

- Develop the ability to prepare a rational argument as preparation for life and employment.

Types of Debate

- Lincoln-Douglas (basic one-on-one debate format)

- Tennis (In teams of three, one student "serves" an opening argument, a student on the other team "returns" through a rebuttal, and so on.)

- Town hall (Students share different perspectives as in a community meeting—we like to split the class between two main perspectives, such as renewable and non-renewable energy sources.)

- Mock trial

- Mock United Nations

Wade's sixth-grade students participating in a United Nations simulation on Human Rights of Refugees with a Captain America vs. Iron Man twist

Tips

- Even first-graders can debate if you choose something that is relevant to them; for example, let them stage a mock trial based on a fairy tale by focusing on textual evidence from the story.

- Start by teaching the format of the debate, maybe with a non-academic topic like *Who's a better superhero—Batman or Superman?* so kids can get the structure down.

- Incorporate your students' interests. We did a mock United Nations exercise based on the premise of a zombie apocalypse.

- Remember the Rules of Rigor: Find a role for every student so no one is sitting it out and listening.

Effective Questioning

What It Is

A means of engaging students and making lessons more active while building student confidence.

Purpose

- Develop critical thinking skills.
- Encourage class participation.
- Build confidence.

Tips

- When you're calling on random students to answer a question, don't set them up to feel embarrassed or inadequate.

- Using a call and response can give the student who's on the spot a chance to compose herself and think. We use the call,

"Meagan has the floor!" And the students respond with, "*Ooooh,* track her!"

- We don't recommend using the "phone a friend" approach to let a stuck student ask for help. When you give students a pass, you're not taking the pressure off—you're showing them that they failed, while all the students with their hands up know the answer.

- Don't let other students raise or wave their hands in the air to show they know the answer while another student is stuck on it. Set that expectation and stick to it.

Wade's fifth-grade students taking ownership of their learning through effective questioning

- Remember, the level of the question asked determines the level of thinking the student must rise to. Instead of calling on someone else, break the question down into simpler components until the student is unstuck and can answer. You essentially show him how to find the answer in as many steps as are necessary, making the final answer a giant victory instead of a flop.

- This approach usually helps a lot of other students who weren't called on but don't know the answer either.

STEM / STEAM

What It Is

A curriculum or lesson plan that incorporates science, technology, engineering, and mathematics in an interdisciplinary and applied approach rather than as four separate topics. (The *A* adds "Arts" to the formula).

Purpose

- Implement hands-on learning through creating, designing, and inventing.

- Develop critical thinking skills.

- Make application of skills and concepts to the real-world.

- Build a learning environment based on inquiry.

- Use group projects to help students develop collaboration skills and expose them to multiple perspectives about solving a challenge.

Tips

- All students should be individually accountable for their own work.

- Try to arrange groups to include participants with different strengths and weaknesses.

- Step away! Allow students to learn from their mistakes and failures.

Socratic Seminar

What It Is

A formal discussion based on a text during which a leader asks open-ended questions, and students listen closely to the comments of others in order to articulate their own responses. Best for middle school and high school, it can be used with any subject.

Purpose

- Develop reading comprehension skills.

- Develop critical thinking skills. (Students must generate and express their own ideas.)

- Explore "big thinking" topics.

- Encourage independent study/research.

- Create student-led discussion.

- Develop speaking and listening skills.

- Build a classroom culture of respect for others.

Tips

- The goal of opening questions is to engage all the participants in identifying the main ideas in a text.

- The goal of core questions is to have the participants analyze the seminar text and develop their ideas about it.

- The goal of closing questions is for participants to consider the ideas and values from the text in real-world applications.

- A round robin format is a good way to get all the participants involved at the beginning. Students can go around in a circle to give their answers or try "hoppin' robin," by jumping in when they choose—as long as everyone responds.

Spoken Word

What It Is

A spoken form of poetry with cross-cultural connections. An "outside the box" way to teach language arts and vocabulary.

Purpose

- Build language arts skills along with vocabulary.
- Get students excited about poetry.
- Inspire students to write.
- Encourage self-expression.
- Explore the role of diversity and oral traditions.

Tips

- Bring rap music into the classroom as a form of rhyming literature. (It's poetry with a beat.)
- Hold a poetry jam (spoken performance) or poetry slam (a form of competitive performance poetry like a rap battle).

Drama / Role Play

What It Is

Students or teachers take on the role of a character different from themselves. It can include drama, costumes, simulations, or role-play related to any topic.

Purpose

- Create a memorable learning experience.

- Provide opportunities for students to experience different perspectives.

Tips

- An easy way to change things up is to teach in a costume that is relevant to the lesson.

- If you're wearing a costume to play a character, own it from the moment your students arrive. Don't break character, even to give instructions.

- Combine with debate forms like mock trial, town hall, or U.N.

- Combine with a room transformation.

- If students will be assuming another role, they may need background information—either through self-study and independent research or through classroom instruction.

Combine learning, drama, and fun with a Mock Trial.

Public Speaking

What It Is

A structured opportunity to deliver information to the rest of the class.

Purpose

- Build confidence.

- Help students build speaking skills that include vocal control, eye contact, organizing information in concise ways, etc.

- These will help students grow accustomed to standing and speaking in front of a group of people and develop the skills of organization, eye contact, vocal control, and so on.

Tips

- Build a culture of respectful listening so the speaker doesn't feel vulnerable or judged.

- Try flipping the script so a student teaches the lesson.

- Play "Word Sneak" as a fun way to incorporate vocabulary words into a spoken presentation. (This is a Jimmy Fallon game, and you can do a Google search for examples and ideas.)

Room Transformation

What It Is

A way to change up the classroom décor to bring students into a new (simulated) environment that will set the mood for and support the content.

Purpose

- Drive engagement for difficult or unpopular content.
- Use hands-on learning activities.
- Teach across content in ways that will let your students make real-world connections.

Tips

- If possible, remove desks and chairs from the room or transform them. (We made desks into "Jeeps" for our safari and *Jurassic World* transformations.)
- Find music and sound effects online (try YouTube) to help set the stage.
- Don't get too hung up on the details. Kids don't look for perfection.
- Stay in character the whole time.
- Offer your students something fun to help them get in character. We've used hats, Hawaiian leis, aprons, surgical masks, you name it.
- Shop for materials at dollar stores and thrift stores, borrow items whenever possible, don't be afraid to ask for something to be donated.

Welcome to Jurassic Park! This room transformation takes students on a wild ride!

Summer, Jayla, and Sydney using dinosaurs to understand adaptations

- Start very small to get the hang of it. Hope's early room transformations relied on basic materials like printed tablecloths and wall signs.

Examples

The following five "Set the Stage to Engage" room transformations are listed in order of increasing complexity. These examples provide a basic overview. You can find more examples, videos, and helpful tips for creating room transformation at *SetTheStageToEngage.com*.

1. Spy Lab / Crime Scene Investigation

- *Objectives*—Learn about research and textual evidence. (This is ELA content, but the activity can become cross-curricular by using history or science texts.)

- *Stage*—Stretch white yarn diagonally across the room and plug in several black lights. (The yarn takes on the appearance of laser beams.) Teachers dress like secret service agents (dark pants/blazer, white shirt, tie, dark glasses, earpiece); students wear black "agent" hats (or badges or anything you can acquire inexpensively).

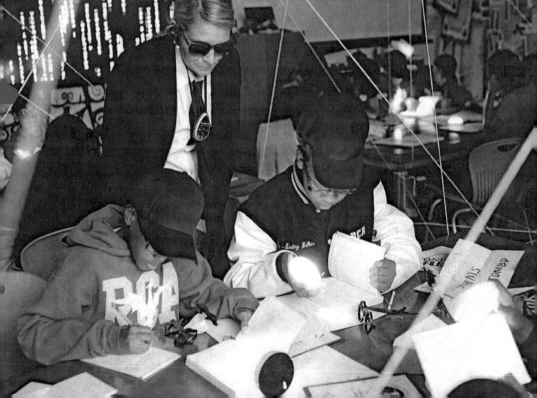

- *Activity*—When students arrive to class, have them wait outside the room to have their fingerprints scanned on "Agent Stone's" phone app. If they are accepted, they can go in and receive their assignment. Stress the idea that the ELA standard of close reading is all about looking for the facts.

2. Pie Face

- *Objectives*—Learn how to identify an author's purpose in a writing passage. Remember different purposes through the acronym PIEED:

  P = Persuade
  I = Inform
  E = Entertain
  E = Explain
  D = Describe

- *Stage*—Set up the Pie Face game on each table, along with a can of whipped cream and five pie tins labeled with the five different purposes (above).

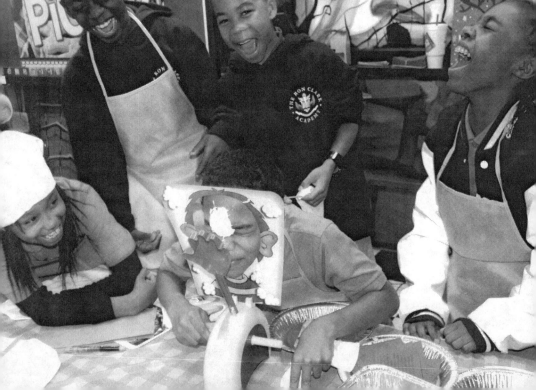

- *Activity*—Split students into groups of four to five kids. All students receive fifteen different passages. Each student reads and looks for patterns and textual evidence to identify the purpose of the writing. After students have identified the purpose, they all present their conclusions to their group. They must each present the textual evidence to support their conclusion. Once they have done that, they "bake their first passage pie" by placing each passage into the correct pie tin— and get to play a round of Pie Face!

3. NASCAR

- *Objectives*—Learn about force and motion by using the scientific process. (Math and ELA activities are added for cross-curricular learning.)

- *Stage*—Decorate the room like NASCAR racing event. Hang checkered flags, set up race tracks with different surfaces, such as sandpaper, tin foil. Teachers wear NASCAR pit crew costumes.

- *Activity*—Students complete experiments on force and motion using the scientific process; for example, students could create and test derby cars made of Legos using balloons to power them. They could test them on different surfaces to learn the effect of friction.

Math: Students time each race and plot it on a graph. They also must find the mean, median, mode, and range.

ELA: Students write a proposal (persuasive essay) and present a speech to four staff members in the school. Their goal is to land a sponsorship for their driver/car. The student with the most points gets to drink milk out of the Winner's Cup (even though that's the Indie 500—we know); plus, they get a trophy.

4. Super Mario and Pirates

- *Objectives*—This room transformation can be used to review ancient civilizations, science studies, math, and ELA topics. It can also be used for cross-curricular reviews.

- *Stage*—Decorate the room with elements reminiscent of a Super Mario video game and wear Mario or Princess costumes. Have the kids wear Mario & Luigi hats. Hang question boxes from the ceiling full of content and questions. Or for a pirate theme, hang torn bed sheets as sails, put treasure chests around the room, and play ocean sounds or the theme song from Pirates of the Caribbean.

- *Activity*—Group students into teams. They will practice a skill that progresses in difficulty, just like the levels of the video game. Each level gets a little harder as each read goes a little deeper. The following example explains how to use the ideas for a reading review, but you can adapt it for any skill.

- **Level 1:** Students must read a passage and interpret each sentence.

- **Level 2:** Students must identify the key idea in shorter passages. In the Super Mario example, students select one of three tunnels. Each tunnel has a different number of passages (between three and eight), which determine how long it takes to complete this level. For a pirate theme, each level is a challenge: fishing for clues, target shooting with Nerf guns. (Do a web search of pirates games for each station.)

- **Level 3:** *Mario Kart!* Students must identify text structures in a passage to help them organize the most important details. The students roll their partner down to the end of the path, collect a short passage, roll them back, decide the text structure, and repeat until the level is complete.

- **Level 4:** *Prize boxes!* The first team to this level breaks open the large box. There are mini question boxes inside. Each team collects one mini box that contains ten different short passages. Have students work together to identify the meaning of unknown words. Once they identify the meaning of each word, they move on to the next level.

- **Level 5:** Students summarize passages. They race down to a tunnel (crawling) to collect a short passage. Then they race back, summarize, and repeat. The students individually work through each level at their own pace. Once the challenge of a level is complete, they move on. They have to complete all five levels to rescue the princess and capture the flag (created using poster board and PVC pipe) or find the hidden treasure.

5. Jurassic Park

- *Objectives*—Learn about life science and ecosystems (animal classifications, adaptations, life cycles, food webs and food chains), by using the scientific method. Integrate math (dodging "disasters" by solving math problems) and ELA (using close reading and comprehension strategies to infer, predict, and draw conclusions about the Jurassic Era).

- *Stage*—Room decorated like *Jurassic Park*, with tables set up as Jeeps, brownie batter used for dinosaur dung. Use pie tins as headlights and insulation pipe as brushguard for the Jeeps. Use giant Easter eggs as dinosaur eggs. Hang black painter's cloth around the room, stage plants in various places, dim the lights and use uplights from the party store to create an outdoorsy feel. Play *Jurrasic Park* music in the background. Teachers wear Jurassic World scientist costumes.

- *Activity*—Students must complete a close reading activity to educate themselves about the Jurassic Period before entering the park. Each student in the Jeep selects a different article. They must then complete four tasks to exit the park.

- *Bonus activity*—Throughout the lesson a warning alarm sounds, and a math problem ("park crisis") pops up on the board. Students must solve the crisis by solving the problem. Every student in the jeep must solve the problem correctly before the team can resume the task they were working on— just to shake things up a bit!

Works Cited

Introduction

Eschleman, Kevin J., Jamie Madsen, Gene Alarcon, and Alex Barelka. "Benefiting from Creative Activity: The Positive Relationships between Creative Activity, Recovery Experiences, and Performance-related Outcomes." *Journal of Occupational and Organizational Psychology,* 87, no. 3 (2014): 579–598. onlinelibrary.wiley.com/doi/10.1111/joop.12064/abstract.

Rentner, Diane Stark, Nancy Kober, and Matthew Frizzell. "Listen to Us: Teacher Views and Voices." *Center on Education Policy.* May 2016. https://www.cep-dc.org/displayDocument.cfm?DocumentID=1456.

Chapter 3

Cameron, Julia. *The Artist's Way.* New York: Random House, 1992.

Chapter 10

Maxwell, John C. "John Maxwell: Leadership Ladder." *Success.* Oct. 9, 2011, success.com/article/john-maxwell-leadership-ladder.

Peterson, Adam. "Ron Clark in MY Classroom! WHAT?!?! TCHRSLRN2 VLOG_095." *Facebook.* facebook.com/adam.peterson.90813/videos/10212958261819379/?fallback=1.

Acknowledgments

There are a number of people without whom this book could never have become a reality. First and foremost, we're overcome with gratitude for Pam and Warren Wheeler, for their presence in our lives and for encouraging us in everything we do. Their unwavering support shaped Hope as she was growing up; they've extended that support to Wade, and to us as a couple. Every day, they encourage us to leave our mark on the world, while holding us accountable to our faith. To both of you: We love you and could not have dreamed of better role models or parents.

Ten years ago, we met Ron Clark and Kim Bearden, whom we are proud to call our friends and mentors. Their influence on our teaching methods began with our first visitation to RCA; two years later, we were fortunate enough to find ourselves working alongside them. Ron first suggested that we write this book; Kim patiently helped us refine and revise early drafts. Ron and Kim: You have motivated us by example. We credit you with shaping us into the educators we are today—and for allowing us to shape young lives, both in South Carolina and in Atlanta. There are no words to express our appreciation for you and the transformative impact you have had on education.

Likewise, we feel indebted to the entire staff, past and present, of the Ron Clark Academy. These are some of the most talented people in the world! They have opened our eyes to the positive benefits of diversity in race, culture, and teaching styles. We often say, *Your vibe is your tribe*, and they have certainly become kin to us. To all of you: Thank you for always having our backs, for making us laugh, and for being ready with a hug whenever we need a pick-me-up.

Our hearts go out to our families and students of the Ron Clark Academy. We could have never had the courage to complete this book without your support. There is nothing more motivating than having our students cheer us on. Moving from a small town to Atlanta, Georgia, was one of the most challenging chapters in our life. You have welcomed us with open arms and have truly made us part of your families.

There are others who have become like family to us on our professional journey. Many thanks to the Lemons family for being our best friends, offering thoughtful advice in life and in faith, holding us accountable to our purpose, and accompanying us in vacation travels to the end of time. We're grateful to Chris Pombonyo for being honest with us when we need to hear hard truths, and for being a loyal friend and a terrific educator who always gives 110 percent. We could not have completed this project without our dear friend Hilda Brucker. She has been a champion for us and we are forever grateful for her. We're also indebted to the entire *Get Your Teach On* team—dedicated educators who inspire us every day and from whom we have learned so much. Thank you all for coming on this journey with us—we appreciate you.

We'll never miss an opportunity to recognize the people who touched our lives at the beginning of our teaching careers. A huge shout out to the staff and families of Pendleton Elementary: You helped us to grow, and the love we have for you—and your community—is forever. Many heartfelt thanks to Dr. Joanne Avery, superintendent of Anderson School District 4. We were so fortunate to have a strong leader who believed in our vision and allowed us to teach creatively in ways we felt passionate about (and who believed that a married couple *can* work together in elementary education). This same level of gratitude extends to Dr. Kevin Black, our beloved Pendleton principal, who always challenged us, mentored us, and supported our creative efforts. Our hats are off to you both. We would not be where we are today without you.

Special thanks to Kirby and Justin Betancourt for the wonderful photos and much-needed assistance with the images and videos for this project—and to Kirk Brown for his creative genius when it came to our ever-changing book cover design.

Finally, we want to acknowledge the special people who helped Wade navigate an especially rocky youth. Profound gratitude goes to Brian Gurley, the youth pastor who provided faith, guidance, and a path forward. Brian, *you* were the wild card. There are others who quite possibly don't realize the impact of their presence on Wade's life, but who kept him going in thousands of ways. These include all the friends from the beach, friends from Anderson University, and the guys in the band—plus their dads (the Reeves family, Jeffcoat family, Collins family, Forest family, Lamonds family, and Wickiser family). To all of you guys, Wade knows in his heart he wouldn't be here today without you. We love you all.

More From

DAVE BURGESS
Consulting, Inc.

Teach Like a PIRATE

Increase Student Engagement, Boost Your Creativity, and Transform Your Life as an Educator

By Dave Burgess (@BurgessDave)

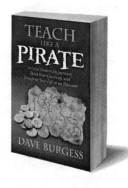

   Teach Like a PIRATE is the New York Times' best-selling book that has sparked a worldwide educational revolution. It is part inspirational manifesto that ignites passion for the profession and part practical road map, filled with dynamic strategies to dramatically increase student engagement. Translated into multiple languages, its message resonates with educators who want to design outrageously creative lessons and transform school into a life-changing experience for students.

Learn Like a PIRATE

Empower Your Students to Collaborate, Lead, and Succeed

By Paul Solarz (@PaulSolarz)

   Today's job market demands that students be prepared to take responsibility for their lives and careers. We do them a disservice if we teach them how to earn passing grades without equipping them to take charge of their education. In *Learn Like a PIRATE*, Paul Solarz explains how to design classroom experiences that encourage students to take risks and explore their passions in a stimulating, motivating, and supportive environment where improvement, rather than grades, is the focus. Discover how student-led classrooms help students thrive and develop into self-directed, confident citizens who are capable of making smart, responsible decisions, all on their own.

P is for PIRATE

Inspirational ABC's for Educators

By Dave and Shelley Burgess (@Burgess_Shelley)

Teaching is an adventure that stretches the imagination and calls for creativity every day! In *P is for PIRATE*, husband and wife team Dave and Shelley Burgess encourage and inspire educators to make their classrooms fun and exciting places to learn. Tapping into years of personal experience and drawing on the insights of more than seventy educators, the authors offer a wealth of ideas for making learning and teaching more fulfilling than ever before.

Play Like a Pirate

Engage Students with Toys, Games, and Comics. Make Your Classroom Fun Again!

By Quinn Rollins (@jedikermit)

Yes! School can be simultaneously fun and educational. In *Play Like a Pirate*, Quinn Rollins offers practical, engaging strategies and resources that make it easy to integrate fun into your curriculum. Regardless of the grade level you teach, you'll find inspiration and ideas that will help you engage your students in unforgettable ways.

eXPlore Like a Pirate

Gamification and Game-Inspired Course Design to Engage, Enrich, and Elevate Your Learners

By Michael Matera (@MrMatera)

Are you ready to transform your classroom into an experiential world that flourishes on collaboration and creativity? Then set sail with classroom game designer and educator Michael Matera as he reveals the possibilities and power of game-based learning. In *eXPlore Like a Pirate*, Matera serves as your experienced guide to help you apply the most motivational techniques of gameplay to your classroom. You'll learn gamification strategies that will work with and enhance (rather than replace) your current curriculum and discover how these engaging methods can be applied to any grade level or subject.

The Innovator's Mindset

Empower Learning, Unleash Talent, and Lead a Culture of Creativity

By George Couros (@gcouros)

The traditional system of education requires students to hold their questions and compliantly stick to the scheduled curriculum. But our job as educators is to provide new and better opportunities for our students. It's time to recognize that compliance doesn't foster innovation, encourage critical thinking, or inspire creativity—and those are the skills our students need to succeed. In *The Innovator's Mindset*, George Couros encourages teachers and administrators to empower their learners to wonder, to explore—and to become forward-thinking leaders.

Master the Media

How Teaching Media Literacy Can Save Our Plugged-in World

By Julie Smith (@julnilsmith)

Written to help teachers and parents educate the next generation, *Master the Media* explains the history, purpose, and messages behind the media. The point isn't to get kids to unplug; it's to help them make informed choices, understand the difference between truth and lies, and discern perception from reality. Critical thinking leads to smarter decisions—and it's why media literacy can save the world.

The Zen Teacher

Creating FOCUS, SIMPLICITY, and TRANQUILITY in the Classroom

By Dan Tricarico (@TheZenTeacher)

Teachers have incredible power to influence—even improve—the future. In *The Zen Teacher*, educator, blogger, and speaker Dan Tricarico provides practical, easy-to-use techniques to help teachers be their best—unrushed and fully focused—so they can maximize their performance and improve their quality of life. In this introductory guide, Dan Tricarico explains what it means to develop a Zen practice—something that has nothing to do with religion and everything to do with your ability to thrive in the classroom.

Lead Like a PIRATE

Make School Amazing for Your Students and Staff

By Shelley Burgess and Beth Houf
(@Burgess_Shelley, @BethHouf)

In *Lead Like a PIRATE*, education leaders Shelley Burgess and Beth Houf map out the character traits necessary to captain a school or district. You'll learn where to find the treasure that's already in your classrooms and schools—and how to bring out the very best in your educators. This book will equip and encourage you to be relentless in your quest to make school amazing for your students, staff, parents, and communities.

50 Things You Can Do with Google Classroom

By Alice Keeler and Libbi Miller
(@AliceKeeler, @MillerLibbi)

It can be challenging to add new technology to the classroom, but it's a must if students are going to be well-equipped for the future. Alice Keeler and Libbi Miller shorten the learning curve by providing a thorough overview of the Google Classroom App. Part of Google Apps for Education (GAfE), Google Classroom was specifically designed to help teachers save time by streamlining the process of going digital. Complete with screenshots, *50 Things You Can Do with Google Classroom* provides ideas and step-by-step instructions to help teachers implement this powerful tool.

50 Things to Go Further with Google Classroom

A Student-Centered Approach

By Alice Keeler and Libbi Miller
(@AliceKeeler, @MillerLibbi)

Today's technology empowers educators to move away from the traditional classroom where teachers lead and students work independently—each doing the same thing. In *50 Things to Go Further with Google Classroom: A Student-Centered Approach*, authors and educators Alice Keeler and Libbi Miller offer inspiration and resources to help you create a digitally rich, engaging, student-centered environment. They show you how to tap into the power of individualized learning that is possible with Google Classroom.

Pure Genius

Building a Culture of Innovation and
Taking 20% Time to the Next Level

By Don Wettrick (@DonWettrick)

For far too long, schools have been bastions of boredom, killers of creativity, and way too comfortable with compliance and conformity. In *Pure Genius*, Don Wettrick explains how collaboration—with experts, students, and other educators—can help you create interesting, and even life-changing, opportunities for learning. Wettrick's book inspires and equips educators with a systematic blueprint for teaching innovation in any school.

140 Twitter Tips for Educators

Get Connected, Grow Your Professional
Learning Network, and Reinvigorate Your Career

By Brad Currie, Billy Krakower, and Scott Rocco
(@bradmcurrie, @wkrakower, @ScottRRocco)

Whatever questions you have about education or about how you can be even better at your job, you'll find ideas, resources, and a vibrant network of professionals ready to help you on Twitter. In *140 Twitter Tips for Educators*, #Satchat hosts and founders of Evolving Educators, Brad Currie, Billy Krakower, and Scott Rocco, offer step-by-step instructions to help you master the basics of Twitter, build an online following, and become a Twitter rock star.

Ditch That Textbook

Free Your Teaching and Revolutionize
Your Classroom

By Matt Miller (@jmattmiller)

Textbooks are symbols of centuries-old education. They're often outdated as soon as they hit students' desks. Acting "by the textbook" implies compliance and a lack of creativity. It's time to ditch those textbooks—and those textbook assumptions about learning! In *Ditch That Textbook*, teacher and blogger Matt Miller encourages educators to throw out meaningless, pedestrian teaching and learning practices. He empowers them to evolve and improve on old, standard teaching methods. *Ditch That Textbook* is a support system, toolbox, and manifesto to help educators free their teaching and revolutionize their classrooms.

How Much Water Do We Have?

5 Success Principles for Conquering Any Challenge and Thriving in Times of Change

by Pete Nunweiler with Kris Nunweiler

In *How Much Water Do We Have?* Pete Nunweiler identifies five key elements—information, planning, motivation, support, and leadership—that are necessary for the success of any goal, life transition, or challenge. Referring to these elements as the 5 Waters of Success, Pete explains that, like the water we drink, you need them to thrive in today's rapidly paced world. If you're feeling stressed out, overwhelmed, or uncertain at work or at home, pause and look for the signs of dehydration. Learn how to find, acquire, and use the 5 Waters of Success—so you can share them with your team and family members.

Instant Relevance

Using Today's Experiences to Teach Tomorrow's Lessons

By Denis Sheeran (@MathDenisNJ)

Every day, students in schools around the world ask the question, "When am I ever going to use this in real life?" In *Instant Relevance*, author and keynote speaker Denis Sheeran equips you to create engaging lessons *from* experiences and events that matter to your students. Learn how to help your students see meaningful connections between the real world and what they learn in the classroom—because that's when learning sticks.

The Classroom Chef

Sharpen Your Lessons. Season Your Classes. Make Math Meaningful.

By John Stevens and Matt Vaudrey (@Jstevens009, @MrVaudrey)

In *The Classroom Chef*, math teachers and instructional coaches John Stevens and Matt Vaudrey share their secret recipes, ingredients, and tips for serving up lessons that engage students and help them "get" math. You can use these ideas and methods as-is, or better yet, tweak them and create your own enticing educational meals. The message the authors share is that, with imagination and preparation, every teacher can be a classroom chef.

Start. Right. Now.

Teach and Lead for Excellence

By Todd Whitaker, Jeff Zoul, and Jimmy Casas
(@ToddWhitaker, @Jeff_Zoul, @casas_jimmy)

In their work leading up to *Start. Right. Now.,* Todd Whitaker, Jeff Zoul, and Jimmy Casas studied educators from across the nation and discovered four key behaviors of excellence: Excellent leaders and teachers *Know the Way, Show the Way, Go the Way, and Grow Each Day*. If you are ready to take the first step toward excellence, this motivating book will put you on the right path.

The Writing on the Classroom Wall

How Posting Your Most Passionate Beliefs about Education Can Empower Your Students, Propel Your Growth, and Lead to a Lifetime of Learning

By Steve Wyborney (@SteveWyborney)

In *The Writing on the Classroom Wall*, Steve Wyborney explains how posting and discussing Big Ideas can lead to deeper learning. You'll learn why sharing your ideas will sharpen and refine them. You'll also be encouraged to know that the Big Ideas you share don't have to be profound to make a profound impact on learning. In fact, Steve explains, it's okay if some of your ideas fall *off* the wall. What matters most is sharing them.

LAUNCH

Using Design Thinking to Boost Creativity and Bring Out the Maker in Every Student

By John Spencer and A.J. Juliani
(@spencerideas, @ajjuliani)

Something happens in students when they define themselves as *makers* and *inventors* and *creators*. They discover powerful skills—problem-solving, critical thinking, and imagination—that will help them shape the world's future ... *our* future. In *LAUNCH*, John Spencer and A.J. Juliani provide a process that can be incorporated into every class at every grade level ... even if you don't consider yourself a "creative teacher." And if you dare to innovate and view creativity as an essential skill, you will empower your students to change the world—starting right now.

Kids Deserve It!

Pushing Boundaries and Challenging Conventional Thinking

By Todd Nesloney and Adam Welcome
(@TechNinjaTodd, @awelcome)

In *Kids Deserve It!*, Todd and Adam encourage you to think big and make learning fun and meaningful for students. Their high-tech, high-touch, and highly engaging practices will inspire you to take risks, shake up the status quo, and be a champion for your students. While you're at it, you just might rediscover why you became an educator in the first place.

Escaping the School Leader's Dunk Tank

How to Prevail When Others Want to See You Drown

By Rebecca Coda and Rick Jetter
(@RebeccaCoda, @RickJetter)

No school leader is immune to the effects of discrimination, bad politics, revenge, or ego-driven coworkers. These kinds of dunk-tank situations can make an educator's life miserable. By sharing real-life stories and insightful research, the authors (who are dunk-tank survivors themselves) equip school leaders with the practical knowledge and emotional tools necessary to survive and, better yet, avoid getting "dunked."

Teaching Math with Google Apps

50 G Suite Activities

By Alice Keeler and Diana Herrington
(@AliceKeeler, @mathdiana)

Google Apps give teachers the opportunity to interact with students in a more meaningful way than ever before, while G Suite empowers students to be creative, critical thinkers who collaborate as they explore and learn. In *Teaching Math with Google Apps*, educators Alice Keeler and Diana Herrington demonstrate fifty different ways to bring math classes to the twenty-first century with easy-to-use technology.

Your School Rocks … So Tell People!

*Passionately Pitch and Promote the
Positives Happening on Your Campus*

By Ryan McLane and Eric Lowe
(@McLane_Ryan, @EricLowe21)

Great things are happening in your school every day. The problem is, no one beyond your school walls knows about them. School principals Ryan McLane and Eric Lowe want to help you get the word out! In *Your School Rocks … So Tell People!*, McLane and Lowe offer more than seventy immediately actionable tips along with easy-to-follow instructions and links to video tutorials. This practical guide will equip you to create an effective and manageable communication strategy using social media tools. Learn how to keep your students' families and community connected, informed, and excited about what's going on in your school.

Table Talk Math

*A Practical Guide for Bringing Math
into Everyday Conversations*

By John Stevens (@Jstevens009)

Making math part of families' everyday conversations is a powerful way to help children and teens learn to love math. In *Table Talk Math*, John Stevens offers parents (and teachers!) ideas for initiating authentic, math-based conversations that will get kids to notice and be curious about all the numbers, patterns, and equations in the world around them.

Shattering the Perfect Teacher Myth

6 Truths That Will Help You THRIVE as an Educator

By Aaron Hogan (@aaron_hogan)

The idyllic myth of the perfect teacher perpetuates unrealistic expectations that erode self-confidence and set teachers up for failure. Author and educator Aaron Hogan is on a mission to shatter the myth of the perfect teacher by equipping educators with strategies that help them shift out of survival mode and THRIVE.

Shift This!

How to Implement Gradual Changes for MASSIVE Impact in Your Classroom

By Joy Kirr (@JoyKirr)

Establishing a student-led culture that isn't focused on grades and homework but on individual responsibility and personalized learning may seem like a daunting task—especially if you think you have to do it all at once. But significant change is possible, sustainable, and even easy when it happens little by little. In *Shift This!* educator and speaker Joy Kirr explains how to make gradual shifts—in your thinking, teaching, and approach to classroom design—that will have a massive impact in your classroom. Make the first shift today!

Unmapped Potential

An Educator's Guide to Lasting Change

By Julie Hasson and Missy Lennard (@PPrincipals)

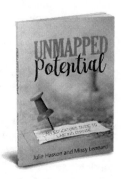

No matter where you are in your educational career, chances are you have, at times, felt overwhelmed and overworked. Maybe you feel that way right now. If so, you aren't alone. But the more important news is that things can get better! You simply need the right map to guide you from frustrated to fulfilled. *Unmapped Potential* offers advice and practical strategies to help you find your unique path to becoming the kind of educator—the kind of person—you want to be.

Social LEADia

Moving Students from Digital Citizenship to Digital Leadership

By Jennifer Casa-Todd (@JCasaTodd)

Equipping students for their future begins by helping them become digital leaders now. In our networked society, students need to learn how to leverage social media to connect to people, passions, and opportunities to grow and make a difference. *Social LEADia* addresses the need to shift the conversations at school and at home from digital citizenship to digital leadership.

Spark Learning

3 Keys to Embracing the Power of Student Curiosity

By Ramsey Musallam (@ramusallam)

Inspired by his popular TED Talk "3 Rules to Spark Learning," this book combines brain science research, proven teaching methods, and Ramsey's personal story to empower you to improve your students' learning experiences by inspiring inquiry and harnessing its benefits. If you want to engage students in more interesting and effective learning, this is the book for you.

Ditch That Homework

Practical Strategies to Help Make Homework Obsolete

By Matt Miller and Alice Keeler
(@jmattmiller, @alicekeeler)

In *Ditch That Homework*, Matt Miller and Alice Keeler discuss the pros and cons of homework, why teachers assign it, and what life could look like without it. As they evaluate the research and share parent and teacher insights, the authors offer a convincing case for ditching homework and replacing it with more effective and personalized learning methods.

The Four O'Clock Faculty

A Rogue Guide to Revolutionizing Professional Development

By Rich Czyz (@RACzyz)

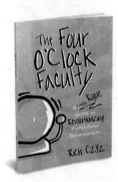

Author Rich Czyz is on a mission to revolutionize professional learning for all educators. In *The Four O'Clock Faculty*, Rich identifies ways to make PD meaningful, efficient, and, above all, personally relevant. This book is a practical guide that reveals why some PD is so awful and what you can do to change the model for the betterment of you and your colleagues.

About the Authors

Hope King is an award-winning educator, blogger, and compulsive crafter. She has a special interest in empowering other teachers, which inspired her to co-found the acclaimed *Get Your Teach On* conference. Hope also distributes original lesson plans and curriculum materials through her blog, *Elementary Shenanigans*, and the "Teachers Pay Teachers" website. She currently teaches reading, language arts, and science to middle-schoolers at the famed Ron Clark Academy in Atlanta, and her innovative methods for driving student engagement there have been showcased. Hope was a recipient of the Debra Peebles Golden Deeds Excellence in Teaching Award by her district. Follow Hope on Twitter (@hopekingteach) and join her on Instagram (elementaryshenanigans).

Wade King serves as the director of curriculum and instruction at the Ron Clark Academy, where he also teaches social studies and current events. His personal passion is using music and debate to drive engagement in the classroom—over 9,000 visiting educators who've observed his teaching methods remember Wade as the teacher with the electric guitar and drum set. Prior to teaching at RCA, Wade was recognized in South Carolina as a District Choice Teacher, Teacher of the Year, and Region Coach of the Year. Wade is a featured presenter at the *Get Your Teach On* conference. Keep up with Wade on Twitter (@wadeking7) and share the fun on Instagram (_wadeking).